Acknowledgment

I express my sincere gratitude to Samantha Simoneau, who once again has used her superior editing talent to make this book a lot better than it would have been if our paths had not crossed. This is the third project on which we have worked together, and that collaboration continues to be a blessing.

Thanks, Sam.

Dedication

To my family, friends, and acquaintances here mentioned - the ingredients for these memories. Thank God for putting us in the right place at the right time.

Foreword

The following stories are true. My wish is that after you read them, you'll take a little time to think about the stories in your own lives. I hope you'll find that many of them reveal moments to hold dear that are worthy of keeping in your hearts.

It was March 5th, 2020, and we were wrapping up our weekly early morning Bible study class. As I sat with my two pals, Howard Miller and 97-year-old Mike Parkar, we discussed where we should go for breakfast. One of the benefits of being an outside salesman for almost 40 years is that I have eaten in just about every diner in the south Jersey-Philadelphia area, and it occurred to me to ask my friends a simple question: "Do you guys like oatmeal?" When they both said yes, I decided to take them to a place in south Philadelphia where the oatmeal was legendary. This dish was so tasty, I put my reputation on the line and *guaranteed* that to taste it would be like dying and going to Heaven! Not many people would drive 20 miles for a bowl of oatmeal, but this was different; it was a culinary adventure, supplemented with the friendly banter that would naturally follow.

The meal did not disappoint. Howard loved it. Upon tasting his oatmeal, Mike's ancient eyes lit up like those of a child with a new toy. (See cover photo.)

Then it struck me... how amazing it was that this simple event could bring such fun and joy to the three of us. That trip, sparked by my impulsive suggestion, gave this wonderful, 97-year-old man a thrill that he frequently laughed and talked about until he peacefully passed away 18 months later.

That breakfast provided a moment to savor, and I came to realize there were many more.

Table of Contents

Acknowledgment iii

Dedication v

Foreword vii

1. Being Prepared 1

2. Before the Numbers...5

3. "Daycare" For a Quarter 8

4. And They're Off! 12

5. Serving the Old Way...17

6. A Battle of Wills..21

7. No Thanks to Man's Best Friend 25

8. The First One Is Special 29

9. Aunt Mildred 33

10. Road Trips, Meals, and Laughter 37

11. The Night I Met "Moses" 42

12. Big Frank 45

13. What's in a Name?..50

14. Checking In 55

15. Honey, I Told You So 60

16. An Ounce of Pandemonium 64

17. Fun in Acapulco?..69

18. Ol' Blue Eyes, Sid, and the Mother's Day Gift 73

19. The Temperamental Discovery 77

20. A Stinging Defeat...81

21. A Friend and a Hero 85

22. Giving Your Heart 90
23. Making the Right Choice 95
24. You Can't Take It With You 98
25. Earning the Bag 102
26. Back on the Road 106
27. A Command Performance...........................112
28. Words Undying 116

1

Being Prepared

"Take that back!"

A LITTLE KID growing up in the city in the '50s learned a few things very quickly. For instance, when you play a game, you'd better try to win. The kids in my southwest Philly neighborhood respected winners, and those who didn't even try were not held in high esteem by their peers. However, if you lost but had made a valiant effort, you gained the respect of everyone. Another fact of life was, sooner or later, you were probably going to be challenged by a kid who was bigger and stronger. That's just the way it was. Back then, bullies didn't use chat rooms, Facebook, or simple insults; they actually got physical. So you had a choice: You either took the abuse, or you stood up for yourself to let the bully know it would be smarter for him to move on to the next kid.

So, when I was about seven years old, my father taught me how to defend myself. It was much worse for him, growing up in the mean streets of south Philly, and he wanted to make sure I was properly prepared to take on my little part of the world.

It wasn't too long before my ability to defend myself was tested. In my neighborhood, you were probably either Italian or Irish. We all usually got along very well, but - every once in a while - someone would utter an ethnic slur, which could easily escalate into juvenile fisticuffs. And that's what happened to me when an older kid on my street called me the magic word that rhymes with "pop," and he was clearly not kidding. Taking offense, I told him to shut up, and then the fun began. He was around three years older than me, and we had an audience of about four other kids. So, when he pushed me, I valiantly tried to hold my own, but his superior size and strength eventually got the better of me.

However, during the fracas, I decided to call upon one of my buddies who I knew could really help in a tough situation. After calling a brief time-out, I removed the Saint Christopher medal from around my neck and squeezed it into my right fist. I doubt whether Catholic doctrine would support my unique use of this blessed medal, but I think Saint Christopher did. After that, I was able to land one or two good rights to the left jaw of my bigger, stronger opponent. Bottom line, I lost the fight on points, but that kid never picked on me again. Atta boy, Saint Chris!

Another time, when I was about nine years old, a bigger kid from around the corner on 65th Street started a fight with me when I wouldn't hand over one of my TastyKake chocolate cupcakes. I barely knew him, and some things in life are worth dying for. Although taller and heavier, the kid wasn't much of a fighter, and he actually cried after our brief contest. During dinner that night, there was a knock on our door. My father worked hard, so interrupting his supper after a long day was not appreciated. However, when Mom answered the door, she called my father over to speak with the visitor, who turned out to be the father of the kid I had fought with a few hours earlier. With his boy at his side, this guy complained to Dad that I beat up his son, so my father called me to the door. After seeing that I was shorter and lighter than his kid, the man asked his son, "Is this the kid who beat you up?" When his son said yes, the old man smacked him in the face, then apologized to my father for wasting his time. That wannabe bully had a bad day. I noticed a suppressed but proud grin on Pop's face as we walked back to the kitchen.

I don't want to give the impression that we were a combative family - we weren't. But that's the way it was in those days. My sister, Kathy, who is almost six years older than me, would routinely tune up her little brother when I got under her skin, which was often. When I reached the age of 10, I was finally stronger than her and could easily handle any physical altercation. My father took me aside, shortly after my tenth birthday, and said, "You don't hit girls."

Talk about being hosed. "She's been kicking my butt for 10 years," I objected, "and now I can't get even?"

He replied, "Life can be tough, Charlie. Get used to it."

Three decades later, I was a happily married father of two. My daughter was eight, and my five-year-old son was about to start kindergarten. Toward the end of summer, just before school began, we were all seated at the dinner table, and our little guy asked, "Dad, what should I do if a bully picks on me at school?" I thought about what Ward Cleaver would say and immediately ruled it out. Instead, I said, "You should never start a fight, but if someone hits you, punch him right in the nose, and he'll never bother you again. You have the right to defend yourself." This horrified the two women in my life. My son replied, "OK, Dad." I taught him how to defend himself, and he never had to punch anyone in the nose. Although a bully did hit him once, and his response was a quick jab to the kid's chest, which promptly ended the fight. No one picked on him again.

That's just the way it is.

2

Before the Numbers

A snowy third-down play

IN THE PHILADELPHIA area, in December of 2017, the winter started off with several minor snowstorms. As I watched the usual hype on TV while the multitude of "correspondence course" meteorologists gave their Armageddon-like forecasts, I couldn't help but remember what it was like back in the '50s, when I was growing up. Great memories popped into my head as I relived how we kids dealt with the gift of a day or two off from school.

First of all, back then, schools didn't have snow-closing numbers to call, and there certainly wasn't "an app for that." If you lived outside of the city, you had to listen for your school's name to be announced, usually on KYW radio. If you lived in the city, you just waited with bated breath to hear the announcer say those magic words, "All Philadelphia public and parochial schools will be closed." In the winter, I made sure to watch the six o'clock news on channel three with anchor Vince Leonard. Vince was OK, but the real reason I watched was to see the hottest weatherman in town, one Wally Kinnan, "the Weatherman." Old Wally was unique because he was a real-life war hero who became a meteorologist and the first one in the country to give his exclusive five-day forecast. This allowed kids like me to look ahead and hope that Wally was on the ball with his prognostications. As a sharp guy who knew how to get ratings, he typically included a mention of snow somewhere in his five-dayer. Early on, however, I realized that Wally's forecast for the fifth day was usually "fair and chilly" - no matter the time of year!

When a snowstorm did close the schools, there were no computers, iPads, or cell phones to stare at while staying nice and warm inside the house. No, we went out into the weather to take full advantage of the unique opportunities for fun that the snow provided. One of our favorite activities was playing tackle football. No one ever got hurt because one couldn't generate any real speed wearing boots and a heavy coat. You could barely run five steps before you either fell on your own or were tackled by one of your buddies. I remember, on multiple occasions, trudging home wet and cold after the game, then making a beeline to the nearest radiator after shedding my wet clothes. The innovation the automobile industry now touts as "seat warmers" must have somehow been stolen from me, since I certainly warmed my "seat" lots of times on top of the radiator.

Before the snow plows were able to take care of Buist Avenue, we would lie in wait for a slow-moving car or truck to approach. Then it was an easy move to grab onto the rear bumper and be towed for a nice ride until the driver stopped. Sometimes they would actually get out and try to chase us, but that always proved fruitless. The best sledding spot was the stretch from Elmwood Avenue to Buist Avenue on 64th Street. If conditions were right, you could enjoy a long, down-hill trip that didn't end until you jumped off of the sled to avoid sliding into traffic at the Buist Avenue intersection.

However, for all of the fun we had outdoors, we also found a way to make the most of the day off *at school*, despite the fact that it was closed. I became friendly with Gene, the cus-todian at our school - Tilden Junior High - who had to report to work even if school was out. After a few phone calls to get some friends together, we would walk to school through the snow and bang on the basement door. Gene was a great guy, so he gladly let us in, turned on the gym lights, and allowed us to play basketball for hours. Back in the early '60s, no one thought about liability lawsuits. He didn't worry about us get-ting hurt, and we would never have told anyone of Gene's graciousness to us, lest he get into trouble.

I'd venture to say that if kids banged on my old school's base-ment door these days, there wouldn't be a guy like Gene around to let them in and provide a venue for some good, clean fun. In fact, someone would probably use a cell phone to call 911 - and that's a shame.

3

"Daycare" For a Quarter

Rodan, the flying monster

BACK IN THE '50s, the good mothers of our southwest Philly neighborhood had the opportunity for a well-deserved break on Saturday afternoons, when two of our local movie theaters offered their much-anticipated matinees. As kids, we looked forward to these shows because they provided us several hours of unsupervised mayhem. Very few of our mothers drove back then, so most of us would walk the seven or eight blocks to Woodland Avenue to join the fun at either the Benn or the Benson Theater.

Both theaters were located on the same 6300 block, but the Benn holds more memories for me than its smaller counterpart. For instance, the Benn offered a 25-cent ticket for those under the age of 13; otherwise it cost 35 cents. My buddy, Tom "Spinner" Manieri was the tallest of our group and, due to an early growth spurt, had to bring his birth certificate as proof that he was indeed younger than 13. The ticket-window attendant at the Benn was an elderly lady who made Spinner prove his age every time he came to a matinee. I once asked her why she couldn't just remember him, but she told me to shut up and mind my own business. Obviously, the Benn management did not force their employees to take a course in sensitivity training.

As soon as we entered the theater, we would always hit the snack counter, and everyone bought a box of popcorn but not just for the nutritional value of the tasty treat inside. The main reason happened *after* the popcorn was consumed. In a darkened theater, the flattened box made an excellent precursor to the modern Frisbee. Once the show started, it took great concentration to actually watch it. There would be so many popcorn boxes flying around, it was nearly impossible to see the onscreen action. Not only that, but, if you were a highly proficient box-flinger, you could actually hit the big screen and puncture it, causing the box to stick in it and dangle. Achieving that degree of marksmanship brought about kudos from those of your buddies who couldn't quite make the grade!

Of course, the theater had a manager - poor guy - whom we nicknamed "Frank Benn," a completely bald man in his 50s. I actually felt bad for him. Someone who knew him said he had a full head of hair before taking that job! Upon our entering, he would be standing there eyeing his soon-to-be nemeses. For us, It was like seeing a condemned man who was about to walk the plank. This fellow was always wearing a clean, white shirt and matching tie upon our arrival, but, by day's end, he looked like he had narrowly escaped a barroom brawl.

This transformation was due to the stressful hours he endured during the matinee. Besides the popcorn-box missiles, Frank had to deal with kids zig-zagging up and down the aisles, incessantly screaming and yelling. Then there were kids who snuck in during the show by opening the emergency doors, Coke and Pepsi spills that caused the floors to be as sticky as fly paper, spitball wars, and other maddening activities, including the occasional minor fistfight. In fact, at least once during the movie, he would have the projectionist shut down the machine and turn on the lights. Then, with the demeanor of a madman, he would charge down the center aisle, screaming out loud while threatening to shut down the theater and throw us all out! This tactic always worked - for about five minutes after the show resumed - and then the bedlam returned with a vengeance, but Frank never did kick us out.

The Saturday matinee really did provide our mothers with a brief respite, and it was always crowded, but the largest crowds seemed to turn up for the horror films with a bunch of cartoons as an appetizer. Without a doubt, the film that attracted the largest audience was *Rodan! The Flying Monster!*, a Japanese film released in the United States in 1957. It was the first Japanese monster movie in color and was taglined, "The most horrifying hell-creature that ever menaced mankind." Yikes! This film depicted a large, flying, prehistoric creature that sprang to life after some miners inadvertently uncovered the wrong mineshaft. This was a classic Japanese movie. The English was poorly dubbed as the residents of Sasebo watched helplessly as their city was being destroyed. Before the theater opened for that show, the line stretched all the way around the corner.

In the annals of Benn Theater folklore, *Rodan* stands out for another reason: That show actually held our interest for about 25 minutes before the first popcorn box was launched - a record that was unbroken throughout my childhood!

4

And They're Off!

The horse that beat the odds

I SUPPOSE SOME of the details are a little fuzzy after all of these years, but the gist of this story would be tough to forget. I recall being about 10 years old at the time. My father and his buddies loved to pick a horse or two each day and place their bets with Tony, the local "entrepreneur," an Italian guy who never wrote anything down on paper. When I asked my father why that was the case, he told me that Tony kept losing his pencils. Even at that tender age, I had an inkling that Tony may have had another reason from which I should be sheltered! At any rate, as the summer approached, my father announced that the family would be attending a Memorial Day picnic with some close friends and Uncle Freddy, Dad's younger brother. The picnic would be held at Delaware Park, a beautiful race track about 15 minutes south of Wilmington off of I-95 and about an hour's drive from our home in southwest Philly. There would be lots of food and fun for the kids while the grownups tried their luck at the ponies.

My uncle was a character. Just a few years younger than my father, Uncle Freddy was affectionately given the nickname "Woodpecker" by my uncle Joe, another brother not in attendance. I wasn't sure why Uncle Joe didn't join us, but it may have had something to do with what Uncle Fred described as his younger brother's "habit of bettin' on slow horses." Uncle Fred's penchant for handing out nicknames (Uncle Joe was "Joe Pierre." My father, Henry, was "Crooch.") and his quick Italian temper, which always made me laugh, were two endearing qualities I greatly appreciated. I also got a kick out of the colorful Italian words that nipped at the heels of his angry but brief tirades!

My mother, Catherine, was a bit of a gambler too, but her game of choice was bingo. She was a legend in the neighborhood and attended about three games a week at our local, ethnic Catholic churches. Mom never played the horses, so Dad's proclamation about the picnic caused her some excitement.

When May 30th rolled around, we hopped in our '57 Dodge Coronet and made the trip to the track. As we arrived and claimed our tables, Mom came over and asked me to pick two horses for her for the "Daily Double," which involved the first two races. The trick was to pick both the winner of the first race *and* the winner of the second race. Once done, you bought a Daily Double ticket that reflected your choices. You had to place your bet on your two picks before the first race started by telling the cashier the number of each horse you chose. Your ticket was only "alive" if your horse won the first race. If it did, you would hold onto your ticket to see if your selection in the second race won. If so, you won the money. The amount you won depended on the payoff for each race, and the higher the odds were against your horses winning, the larger the payoff.

I told Mom to play number eight in the first race and number three in the second. As luck would have it, the number-three horse withdrew, or was "scratched," before the first race even began, so I had to pick another for the second race. I chose number eight, so we had an "eight and eight" Daily Double ticket that cost Mom $2. Our number-eight horse in the first race was named Flo Syrum, who went off at 15-1 odds. These are not good odds for a victory; however, when the race was over …

The winner of the race: ***Flo Syrum!***

Mom, my big sister Kathy, and I were all excited that we had the only "live" Daily Double ticket in our group. Dad shook his head in disbelief of what he just saw, that his little kid got lucky and picked a winner, while all of these old guys - who read the racing forms and studied, or "clocked," the entries - ended up picking losers. Then the real drama began. The number-eight horse I chose for the second race was named White Bait. As the horses came out onto the track to warm up, we got our first glimpse of my pick. White Bait looked like he was ready, right after the race, to hop into the truck for a ride to the nearest Elmer's glue factory. He was a pale beige color, and his neck flailed back and forth as he trotted out. Everyone at our table was silently aghast at his appearance, except Uncle Freddy, who almost fell off of the bench with laughter as he shouted, "Look at that nag you picked!" The betting public must have agreed because White Bait went off at 50-1 odds.

As our horse entered his number-eight position in the starting gate, he seemed to settle down some. When the race began, White Bait took off as if chased by demons. He led all the way, and, as he came to the final few hundred yards - or the "stretch" - he was in a nose-to-nose battle with the number-five horse, who was the favorite at 5-2 odds. Our table was positioned right at the finish line. As White Bait raced with his whole heart and soul, both horses crossed the line simultaneously. My father said, "Oh, my God, he got beat by a nose in a photo finish." Uncle Fred's mouth was open, but he was no longer laughing. We all stood in shock until the official result was announced after the photo was developed. My father was a very smart guy and usually right about most things.

But not that day! It was White Bait by a nose!! The Daily Double payoff to Mom for her $2 bet? $758.80!!

After the initial hootin' and hollerin', I approached dear Uncle Fred with a smile and said, in my most macho 10-year-old voice, "Whaddya think of that nag now, Woodpecker?!" He just smiled and gave me a hug, saying, "Atta boy, Charlie."

Mom spent the money on some much-needed new furniture from Wanamaker's, but not before she gave me my cut, a crisp $5 bill, which was icing on the cake to me and more money than I could possibly need at a time when movies cost 25 cents, and Tastykakes were a dime! Besides, the thrill of victory was payment enough.

As I said, some of the details may be a little fuzzy, but I sure remember most of the best ones!

5

Serving the Old Way

Votive candles that really burn

AT LEAST YOU'D have to say that I'm consistent. As I get older, I often realize that there are many things I prefer the way they once were. I like baseball without the "designated hitter," the "closer," and the eighth-inning "set-up man." I don't like giving out participation trophies to everyone who happens to show up, instead of only to those who excel. Lastly, being a Roman Catholic who attends church regularly, I happen to prefer the Mass the way it used to be when I was a kid.

When I was about eight years old, a few of my buddies and I decided to become altar boys. We figured it would look really good on our résumés when it came time to make our way through the pearly gates. Today, both boys and girls can become *altar servers*, since the rules changed in 1983, and girls were allowed to participate. Back then, as now, it was considered an honor to serve during the Mass by assisting the priest as he carried out the age-old duties during that holy hour. It was a blessing I thoroughly enjoyed, and - as with most things in my life - serving at Our Lady of Loreto Church, at 62nd and Grays Avenue in southwest Philly, provided more than a few memories worth sharing.

Right off the bat, becoming an altar boy presented a challenge, primarily because, back then, the Mass was said completely in Latin, which meant all of the candidates had to memorize many prayers and responses in a foreign language. Thankfully, most of the responses were short ones, with the exception of the Confiteor. This prayer of more than 100 words had to be mastered before you earned your wings, so to speak.

Then there were the everyday issues that tested my resolve, like serving at the 6:00 a.m. daily Mass. Doing so required awakening at 4:30 and walking six blocks to church with no breakfast because, at the time, one had to fast from midnight in order to receive Holy Communion. I was always hungry when I left the house, but that wasn't the worst part of the trip. Directly across from our church stood Mattera's Bakery, so, as I rounded the corner at 63rd and Grays, I could smell the fresh bread baking. The fact that the bakery was across from our church was more than fitting, since the fragrance - to this hungry, sleepy eight-year-old - was indeed heavenly! By the time I climbed the church steps, I was starving and couldn't wait to receive the sacrament of Holy Communion, the blessed host for both spiritual and physical nourishment. As soon as Mass was over, I would run across the street to buy a fresh, hot roll for three cents to devour on the way home. To me, that mini meal was worth a million dollars.

If you were lucky enough, the priest would assign you to a wedding. I say "lucky" because serving at a wedding usually meant that you would receive a tip from either the bride's father or the groom. In fact, one of the veteran servers took me aside to tell me that you could be rewarded pretty well, depending on how you did your job. At first I wasn't quite sure what he meant, but I soon learned that the tips were directly proportionate with how happy you looked during the wedding Mass. One time, after a wedding, I received a tip from the groom, followed 10 minutes later by another from the bride's father. I strategically chose to believe that both were gifts from two very generous gentlemen rather than the result of mixed signals.

Then there was the time when my partner, Johnny, and I served at the most attended Mass, 9:00 a.m. on Sunday. The priest's name was Father Veneziale, a short, husky man who spoke with a heavy Italian accent that made understanding his English impossible. When he officiated at the daily Masses, he delivered his homilies in Italian. Since those Masses were mostly attended by the elderly parishioners, his Italian was easily understood. However, on this Sunday, when Johnny and I served, he would speak to the congregation - made up of mostly kids with some adults - in his broken English. As Father walked to the podium to begin his homily, John and I took our seats, which were two folding chairs just inside the communion rail, next to the bank of votive candles. I could tell that Johnny was a little tired by the sluggish way he had been performing his duties thus far. I figured the break in the action and the little rest while Father spoke would provide Johnny his second wind, but what happened next was anything but relaxing.

About 10 minutes into the sermon, I heard a noise that sounded like snoring. I glanced to my left in time to watch as a sleeping Johnny tumbled into the lit candles, and he was still snoring! His surplice - the shirt-like linen vestment we wore over our gown-like cassock - caught fire. Two of the male ushers immediately vaulted over the rail and smothered the flame with their suit jackets. Johnny was unhurt and, by then, very awake! Father Veneziale was shocked. Looking out into the congregation, I saw two of my friends in the second row, giggling. When I turned back to Johnny, we both started laughing. It was a Mass to remember.

I'm sure it is highly unlikely that I'll see an altar server's vestments catch fire during Mass again. Today, thank God, the "candles" are mostly battery operated.

6

A Battle of Wills

"Oh, no, fish again."

MY UNCLE, JOE Sacchetti, and his wife, Aunt Pauline, struggled like most parents back in the '50s in their efforts to raise their two sons, Chris and Joe Jr. Uncle Joe was a hardworking man who held many jobs and always found a way to support his family. He was the third eldest of his siblings, born in 1919, and he passed away at 80. To mention a few of Uncle Joe's jobs, he worked for the railroad; delivered milk, butter, and eggs to homes in the wee hours of the morning; drove various trucks; worked as a longshoreman; and even rode the south Philly streets selling fruits and vegetables as a proverbial "huckster." Suffice it to say Uncle Joe knew how to make a buck. During their 50-plus years of marriage, my aunt and uncle tried to stretch every dollar as they shared their lives in a tiny row home on the 700 block of Watkins Street.

Like all good Italian-American "housewives" at the time, Aunt Pauline managed her home and, as a devout Catholic, dutifully enforced the "no meat on Fridays" rule, which usually meant that whatever fish was on sale that week became Friday's dinner. This was no problem with three of the four family members. Uncle Joe and Aunt Pauline liked fish. Cousin Chris - a big, strong kid and the oldest boy by 18 months - would eat just about anything, but Joey was a different story. He hated fish, often lobbying his mom to replace it with pasta e fagioli or anything else that didn't live in the ocean.

One particular Friday, when dinner time rolled around, Uncle Joe gave his distinctive whistle - which served as a Neapolitan "dinner bell" - and 13-year-old Joey sprinted home from up the street to sit down to a meal of flounder and string beans. As Chris was busy enjoying the food, Joey said, "I don't want this, Mom. Can you make me some potatoes and eggs?" My aunt had a soft heart for her youngest, so she started to make the requested dish. Uncle Joe was not pleased at all. "What is this kid, a professor?" he asked indignantly. "I'm outside driving a milk truck all day, and he gets treated like he's in a restaurant." Aunt Pauline gave her husband a motherly smile and proceeded to make the special order for her baby.

Uncle Joe calmed down, finished eating, and promptly put

Joey's untouched plate of fish and beans in the refrigerator. He wasn't going away without retribution, however. After dinner, he announced that due to his skillful manipulation of his loving mother, Joey was not permitted to go out with his buddies that night. He was also forbidden to have any additional snacks that evening. This threw a monkey wrench into Joey's plan. The small portion of potatoes and eggs was not nearly enough to satisfy a growing boy's appetite, so Joey was still hungry, and - to make matters worse - he and his buddies had planned to get a pizza at their favorite spot that night. That idea was now a mere fantasy; he was grounded.

When the Saturday morning sun peeked out after a hungry night's sleep, Joey awoke and headed straight for the kitchen. He figured he was the first one downstairs and had the whole place to himself. In actuality, Mom was outside talking to a neighbor, Dad's bedroom door was closed, and Chris was in the shower. A short walk through the tiny hallway was all that stood between him and his coveted bowl of Cheerios. As he grabbed a large bowl and the box of cereal, he heard footsteps. He turned to find his father, my Uncle Joe, standing there, dressed and ready for the breakfast which would fuel his morning huckstering.

"Hi, Pop."

"Hi, kid. You hungry?"

"Sure am; those potatoes and eggs didn't fill me up."

"Oh, good. I've got the perfect thing."

With that, Uncle Joe marched to the refrigerator, removed the plate of fish and string beans, and said:

"*Mangiare.* Pass me the bowl and the Cheerios."

It seems that while young Joey proved victorious in the great "potatoes and eggs" caper the night before, he was outflanked by the general in that little Watkins Street kitchen the next morning. And, inexplicably, the second in command, Aunt Pauline, was not around to come to Joey's aid. Her temporary "deployment" at her neighbor's house was a brilliant tactic.

7

No Thanks to Man's Best Friend

On the loose in southwest Philly

IN OUR SOUTHWEST Philly neighborhood, during the late '60s, not many of my buddies had their own car. Most of us had driver's licenses, but, in order to use them, we usually had to rely on the generosity of our parents in letting us borrow the family car. But one of my friends had a strong independent streak, so he was the first one to go out and get himself a set of wheels. My buddy, Ronny Wagner, had worked hard to save money earned from his summer and after-school jobs and took the plunge by buying a 1958 Buick. Of course, Ronny had hoped that this tank-like vehicle would open the door to fun and adventure and, as a late teen, his definition of adventure was a date with the girl of his choice. His car was also the means of transportation for the rest of us. Whether it was a trip to a ball game, a movie, a golf driving range, or a restaurant, good ol' Ronny was the captain of our ship.

I, myself, had two incidents involving Ronny's car that have become folklore among our friends and are recounted every now and then some 50 years later. He once let me borrow the car to go to one of my baseball games. It was only about a 10-mile round trip, but it was drizzling, and I thought driving my scooter would be a tad uncomfortable, let alone dangerous, if it really started to rain. The heavy car was difficult to steer and ran sluggishly. Not only that, but I smelled smoke. It wasn't until I returned that Ronny pointed out, with appropriate disbelief, that I had driven the whole way with the emergency brake engaged. It seems that 10-year-old baby didn't have all of its indicator lights working, so how would I know the brake was on? No major harm was done, and, after I pleaded my case, my dear friend forgave the oversight.

However, the second incident was far more serious and could have easily been disastrous. Ronny had been working on getting a date with this particular blonde beauty for weeks. Every time he asked, she was busy, which was very believable given her popularity and obvious feminine charms. But my pal persisted, and, after five fruitless efforts, she finally accepted his invitation to go out on Saturday night. Ronny was thrilled and pulled out all of the stops. He bought a new shirt and slacks. He made a reservation for two at Pagano's, the popular eating spot on the campus of the University of Pennsylvania. Most importantly, he spent all morning that Saturday cleaning his car, inside and out. After he finished, I suggested we take a ride to get lunch. Ronny had expended a lot of energy and worked up a good appetite, so he was up for the idea.

At this point, it is important to note that life was much simpler back in the late '60s. You could leave your doors unlocked at night; people looked out for one another, and we weren't bogged down by a bunch of city ordinances to make life complicated. Speaking of ordinances, there was no leash law back then. It was very common to see a dog or two running around the neighborhood. In fact, the dogs in southwest Philly had good street smarts, but one thing they didn't have was good personal hygiene. When you walked the streets, it was best to keep one eye on the ground, or you risked stepping in something you would not welcome with open arms, so to speak. So when Ronny and I exited the restaurant and got into his sparkling clean '58 Buick that would soon serve as the chariot for his lady love, we looked at each other with alarm as we sat in the front seats. Our faces simultaneously grimaced at the extremely unpleasant, unmistakable odor that suddenly permeated the entire interior. Reflexively, I glanced down at my low-cut, black Converse All-Star sneakers and yelled, "Oh, no, it's on me!"

With only five hours until the big date, Ronny went into attack mode. He scrubbed the mats three times and hung up multiple little pine tree deodorizers. He didn't want my help; it seemed I had perhaps done enough. When the young lady entered the car, it was the moment of truth - she sat down and only remarked that the pine fragrance was a little too much. After rolling down the window, she was fine. Ronny's quick actions and extraordinary cleaning techniques averted what very easily could have been a dating disaster. As he breathed a sigh of relief, Ronny thought those little pine trees were worth their weight in gold.

8

The First One Is Special

The author with LuAnn and baby Rosie

AS I WAS going through some old papers a while ago, I found a document that immediately took me back to a very special time in my life. It was a certificate of copyright registration that I obtained in 1981. At the time, I never anticipated becoming an author and certainly had no idea that something called the internet would emerge, allowing me to regularly post my essays. I was just a young dad who wanted to write a piece that my firstborn child, our little girl, would someday read with fondness and still feel the love. I thought it would be neat to get it copyrighted, so I did.

Looking back, over 40 years later, I still remember much of what it feels like when two young people are expecting the arrival of their firstborn. In my case, I'd describe it as "controlled terror." The thought of another mouth to feed, along with the responsibilities of protecting and providing, seemed quite intimidating for someone like me, who chooses to approach life in a lighthearted manner. I was thrilled to have the baby on the way, but every now and then the enormity of the arrival would make me come back to earth.

Back in 1979, I carried a beeper for my job. As there were no cell phones in those days, and I was on 24-hour call, I took the pager home with me each evening. It only beeped; there was no voice capability. Whenever it beeped, I found a phone and called a predetermined number at my office. I then received my message. I had the bright idea of giving my wife, LuAnn, this special way of contacting me, in case she needed me. I gave her a spare beeper, and we agreed that she was only to page me if she was ready to deliver. If I heard it, the game plan was that I would drop everything and race home to take her to the hospital. The baby was due around June 19th. I used to play a lot of tennis in those days, and it was on Memorial Day, May 30th, when I was about to hit a backhand, and I heard it: *beep, beep, beep!* I had to assume the baby was about to join us.

As I drove like a maniac to get home to Drexel Hill, Pennsylvania, about eight miles away, I came to West Chester

Pike and drove directly into a parade, nearly mowing down a frightened tuba player. Leaping from the car, I screamed to a cop that my wife was having a baby, and I had to get home. He stopped the whole parade, allowing me to cross the highway, and wished me good luck as I thanked him between hyperventilations. When I rushed into the house, I saw my lovely, very pregnant wife calmly running the vacuum cleaner at the top of the stairs. When she asked me why I was home so early, I realized that I was the victim of a malfunctioning beeper. We both laughed. Happily, LuAnn presented me with our daughter, Rosanne, on June 26th. She arrived about a week late, but it was a very special day for another reason: It happened to be my 32nd birthday. She is, by far, the best birthday present I have ever received. By the way, her delivery occurred with no help from the infamous beeper; we were home together when the contractions reached the critical stage.

It's funny how you remember events that only took a second or two to occur. For me, I'll never forget the look on baby Rosie's face when she tasted spaghetti and her mother's gravy for the first time. She was just five months old, and her eyes widened and lit up as if to ask, "Where're the meatballs?" I suppose being born on your dad's birthday somehow makes you destined to be at least a little like your father. That's certainly the case here, since Rosie and I share a penchant for good times; good friends; good Italian food; and, of course, the Phillies - who can be good or bad!

So, after I saw that copyright document, I decided to take another look at the poem I wrote back in 1981, just before Rosie's second birthday. I'd had it written out by a calligrapher and professionally framed for posterity. It had been quite a while, years even, since I had read the poem. I wondered if doing so would still stir up those wonderful feelings, as it always had done in the past.

It did.

FOR ROSANNE

The beauty of her being is there for us to hold.
Her smile as she awakens, both innocent and bold.
She'll steal your heart but give you hers in such a special way.
And she knows we love her more with every passing day.

Her mother's hair, her father's eyes, His special recipe.
The look upon her frowning face when tears replace the glee.
A giggle here, a giggle there, then on your lap she'll lay.
And she knows we love her more with every passing day.

Oh, when she's grown and has her own, she'll come to realize
That she feels then, as we do now, there are the binding ties.
Then one night, with hand held tight, she'll smile, and then
she'll say,
"Child of mine, I love you more with every passing day."

Daddy
6-21-81

9

Aunt Mildred

1968 Buick Electra 225

IN 1962, AT the tender age of 15, I decided to adopt someone. Of course, the adoption was neither official nor legally binding, but an adoption it was. You see, I decided to take my buddy Brian Schwartz's aunt Mildred as my own, despite the fact that her first encounter with me wasn't very pleasant. In fact, she figured I was a troublemaker and couldn't wait to let me have it! I had gotten my hands on some Tilden Junior High stationery and sent some very official-looking letters to a few of my friends. The bogus congratulatory letters informed the guys that they had been elected to the Tilden Junior High Academic Hall of Fame and would be honored at an upcoming banquet. It was really done for laughs, but when she read the letter, Mildred took the bait and was thrilled that her nephew would receive such an honor. When Brian broke it to her that it was just one of my pranks, she wondered aloud, "What kind of kid would do something like this?" She found out pretty soon because I met her a few days later, and it was love at first sight. After we spoke for about 15 minutes, she realized I wasn't a sociopath after all and proceeded to "punish" me with a piece of her triple-layer chocolate cake.

Throughout high school and college, my adopted aunt and I stayed close. Mildred was Brian's dad's sister, and she spent a lot of time at Brian's house with his mom, Lucille. My pal and I were fixtures at each other's homes and took full advantage of each other's cultural cuisine. During the Jewish holidays, I never missed a Rosh Hashanah dinner at Brian's house, and he was a frequent Sunday guest at our home for our traditional 1:00 p.m. Italian meal.

After I was married, my wife, LuAnn, became great friends with Mildred. Our two kids called her "Aunt Mildred," and she loved them as if they were her own. In fact, the night our son was born, it was Mildred who stayed with our three-year-old, Rosie, while we were at the hospital waiting for the new baby. As the kids grew, we visited Mildred's apartment on many occasions, and she always had a delicious treat for us when we arrived. She was a fabulous cook but an even better baker. Nothing topped her cherry cheesecake, which was in a class of its own. We were like family right up until the day she died. Although life threw her more than a few curveballs, Mildred always kept her sense of humor, and her heart grew more tender as the years rolled by. She was kind in many different ways; however, one example of her kindness to me stood out from all others, and it happened in 1968.

At the age of 21, I was a college student living at home without my own wheels. The lack of my own vehicle was never really an issue, since my dad usually allowed me the use of his 1963 Ford Fairlane for any dates I was able to set up. I had been anxiously awaiting the upcoming Saturday night, when I would have my first date with a very cute, blonde, fellow Temple University student. It was a beautiful June day, and the night promised to be equally lovely. Brian and I were at my house that afternoon, and, at 1:00, I casually mentioned to my dad that I needed the car that evening, taking for granted that it would be available. When Dad told me no because he and Mom were going out, I couldn't believe two things:

- First, that they were actually going out on their favorite TV night, which they usually spent watching *Bonanza* and snacking on Mom's homemade pizza at 8:00 p.m.
- Second, that I could be so stupid as to not make sure the car would be available before setting up this date that I worked so hard to get.

Upset by the disturbing news, I reacted like any mature young adult would: I angrily attempted to negotiate with Dad to change his plans. In fact, I was acting disrespectfully, which could make my car problem pale in comparison to what Dad might do to straighten me out, 21 or not. As Brian looked on, I finally gave up and decided to go out. I yelled to my mother in the kitchen, "Bye, Mom," and proceeded toward the front door, deliberately ignoring my father. With that, Dad sprang from his chair, and Brian ran from the house, leaving me alone to quickly apologize for my childishness… Which I did!

As I drove Brian back to his house aboard my Vespa, I tried to think of a good excuse to break my date but came up with nothing. Upon arriving at Brian's house, I noticed that Mildred was visiting. She took one look at me and perceptively asked what was wrong. When I related the story to her, she smiled and said, "You can take our car." To just call it a "car" was an injustice, as it happened to be a perfect, powder blue, 1968 Buick Electra 225 convertible. I was off the hook, and my would-be embarrassing evening was turned into a great time as my date and I cruised the streets of Philadelphia in style, compliments of my sweet aunt Mildred.

10

Road Trips, Meals, and Laughter

The cookie caper

I HAVE OFTEN said that my time as a baseball player at Temple University was a blessing in many ways. Not only were we very successful record-wise, which is always the number-one goal of any team, but we also shared experiences and camaraderie which still evoke wonderful memories after all these years. Certainly the victories, especially the ones that led to championships, are forever imprinted in my mind, but running a close second are those times of mirth and laughter that happened off the field of play. As I look back, I realize that those fun times often occurred when we were away from home and in a restaurant.

I vividly recall the season of 1969, my senior year and final year of eligibility. I had been looking forward to our trip to the University of Pittsburgh, where we were scheduled to play a Saturday doubleheader. The main reason for my excitement was that we were going to play in Forbes Field, the home of the Pittsburgh Pirates. Although I had played several games at Connie Mack Stadium, the home of the Phillies, I had not yet played in any other Big League park. As a second baseman, it would be a thrill to play that position on the same turf that the Pirates' second baseman, Bill "Maz" Mazeroski, patrolled for so many years. When we embarked on the long bus ride Friday evening, I thought of Maz turning all of those double plays and hitting that World Series-winning home run just nine years earlier. Unfortunately, it started raining on the Pennsylvania Turnpike and didn't stop until the next day at 2:00 p.m., when we left to go home. Our doubleheader was rained out, and the games at Forbes were not meant to be.

However, it wouldn't be a total loss because our coach, Skip Wilson, told us that we would be visiting the famous smorgasbord restaurant, the Collegeville Inn, for dinner. The only problem was that we had not made reservations for our group of 25. Skip told us to go inside in groups of three or four, but, by the time we arrived, we were all starving, so Skip's tactical approach went by the wayside as youthful hunger overtook good sense. We stormed the place! The Skipper's idea probably wouldn't have worked anyway, since we were all wearing our maroon Temple University blazers and were instantly identified as a large group by the slightly overwhelmed, yet accommodating, restaurant manager.

While in the restaurant, we feasted on such delicacies as baby lobster tails, crab meat with drawn butter, steak, chicken, and about 50 other dishes. It was as if the locusts had descended upon the crops. About an hour into the meal, a waiter brought out a giant dish of strawberries. When one of our burly pitchers heard a teammate say, "Look, strawberries," the pitcher turned abruptly and lunged toward the fruit, knocking over a little old lady, who was caught by our third baseman, saving the day. It was one of the best catches of his career. Soon, after a quiet but tense consultation with the manager, the coach approached us and announced that dinner was over, and we had to leave… immediately.

Another time, in 1968, when we were on our way home from a victory over Princeton, we stopped for dinner at a pre-planned destination on Route 1, not far from the university. The meal was rather uneventful - nothing like the Collegeville invasion. We had two long tables set up and were seated and served by a staff that was obviously used to handling team meals. I was sitting next to one of my best friends, an out-fielder about my size, 5'10", but he had a legendary appetite and was known to have eaten three dishes of spaghetti at one sitting. I know because it was Mom's spaghetti one Sunday when he was our guest. He was smart enough to use his eating prowess for fun and profit, winning many bets against those who ignorantly questioned his ability.

After our meal, it was time for dessert, and all 10 guys at

my table ordered ice cream. When I saw the huge scoop of vanilla on my buddy's dish, I said to him, "I'll bet you a dollar that you can't put that whole scoop of ice cream in your mouth at once and eat it." Naturally, all of the guys egged him on, hooting and hollering. Our other table joined in, as did a few of the local patrons, so my friend succumbed to peer pressure and took the bet. As soon as he put all that ice cream into his mouth, his eyes became as big as golf balls, and he made sounds that I had never heard before. I almost regretted being the instigator of this sub-freezing torture, tempting him with that dollar, but the laughter his discomfort provided to the whole team squelched my emerging guilt. So let's just say that everybody won! He earned the money, his legend grew, and it was one of the best dollars I've ever spent!

There is one other story that still makes me laugh every time it crosses my mind. It was 1967, and we were at Penn State the night before we were to play a Saturday doubleheader. One of my teammates, Steve Pitler, was from Norfolk, Virginia. More than just a great teammate, Steve was a terrific athlete and a rarity in that he was letterman in three different collegiate sports: baseball, football, and wrestling. A big, strong guy who stood at 6'2" and weighed about 230 pounds, Steve had another quality that made him special to me: He had the driest sense of humor and could really crack me up. Since he was our first baseman, and I played second base, we were always right next to each other during games. That was an adventure because he would even say hilarious things during the games that kept me more than "loose."

His dad drove up to Penn State to watch the games, so Steve borrowed the family car and took a few of us into town to grab a bite to eat. We went to a little local restaurant and sat at the counter to enjoy our meal. When we were finished, we all headed for the register to pay our checks. The cashier was an elderly lady of about 75 and appeared to have a sweet grandmother's demeanor. I approached her first, and, as I was paying, I looked at the pastries on display in the glass case below the counter. I happen to love peanut butter cookies, so when I thought I spotted some, I asked the grandmotherly lady if they were, in fact, my favorite kind.

She went *nuts*!

"Granny" screamed at me, saying, "No, they aren't peanut butter; they're oatmeal! Can't you see the difference? You college kids drive me crazy." At that point, I had decided that she *was* crazy but chose not to say so and just calmly paid my bill while she caught her breath. The other two guys paid, and then it was Steve's turn. Big Steve lumbered up to the counter and asked, in the sweetest southern tone, "May I please have one of those cookies, Ma'am?" The lady gave Steve the cookie and took his money. He smiled politely, took a bite of the cookie, and said, "Boy, these sure *taste* like peanut butter cookies." I nearly fell over laughing as the cashier stood - speechless, stunned, and staring - while the last remnant of sanity left her.

There is a saying: Timing is everything. Well, Steve always had good timing when he was hitting, but it was never better than his timing that night at the cookie counter.

11

The Night I Met "Moses"

Charlton Heston at his best

LET'S FACE IT: You never know how you will act if you come in contact with greatness. I found out in June of 1972, at a hotel in Omaha, Nebraska. As the 25-year-old Business Manager of Athletics at Temple University, I had the honor of planning all aspects of our baseball team's trip to the College World Series. Back then, the series venue was Rosenblatt Stadium in Omaha. Temple had earned the right to compete against seven other teams for the national championship by defeating Long Island University and Penn State at the NCAA District II regional playoffs hosted by Princeton University.

You could feel the excitement in the air as we checked into the hotel upon our arrival. It was a stately facility, the kind that reminds you of hotels in the old movies, with glittering chandeliers and a mahogany front desk. The massive lobby boasted overstuffed leather sofas and chairs, along with an abundance of hand-carved oak tables.

That evening would feature the Welcoming Dinner, hosted by NCAA officials providing festivities to honor the eight participating teams and their various entourages. As I waited in the lobby for dinner time, I decided to pick up the local newspaper, sink into one of those plush leather chairs, and find out what else was going on in cornhusker land. Nothing really grabbed my attention, except for the story about a celebrity who was in town to speak at a local college - none other than the great Charlton Heston, one of the biggest movie stars in Hollywood. Heston had won the Oscar for best actor in the epic movie *Ben-Hur,* which was awarded a total of 11 Oscars, including best picture. Among other films, he starred in another epic, *The Ten Commandments,* in which he gave a stunning performance as the biblical hero Moses.

After reading the Heston piece, I flipped over to the sports page to see what was being said about our series. Within seconds, I heard a shuffling sound and looked up. I was amazed to see an imposing, 6'3", broad-shouldered, impeccably dressed man carrying an attaché case and walking directly toward me. Incredibly, it was him - Charlton Heston in the flesh.

As a carefree, fun-loving 25-year-old, I guess I had never really considered how I would react if a living legend should ever approach me. I suppose I could have graciously walked up to him, offered my hand, and introduced myself. I could have quietly glanced at him, awed by this accomplished man's fame and achievements. I could have even politely told him how much I admired his work and asked for his autograph. Instead, I just did what came to me in the moment: I stood up, extended my arms out to the sides, and said in a moderately loud, somewhat theatrical voice, "Moses!"

The great Charlton Heston gave me a look that was a cross between a smirk and a wry smile and simply kept walking. I got the impression that perhaps it wasn't the first time he had heard that remark. I know he did in *The Ten Commandments!* But, this time, it was delivered by me, and that experience has provided me with a memorable story, making me smile for nearly 50 years.

12

Big Frank

Cousin Frank's tomato pie

WHEN I WAS growing up in Philly, I thought it was pretty cool that we had a bunch of cousins who lived in Rhode Island, all from my paternal grandmother's side of the family. Whenever we drove north to see them, or they came to visit, there was always fun to be had.

My earliest recollections of our trips to the Warwick area are from when I was about seven years old. I remember visiting with a bunch of my father's cousins, who greeted us with love, food, and laughter. My dad had a good time teasing them about their New England accents, and they gave as good as they got. They were mostly my parents' age and were all very interesting. One cousin owned a factory that manufactured costume jewelry, and he lived in a large, beautiful rancher in Barrington overlooking the Narragansett Bay. His brother was a priest. Two of our cousins were unmarried sisters who were also well off and actually had a golden piano in their living room. Another cousin, whom we called "Sonny," was a brilliant psychology professor at Brown University. When I found out that he used hypnosis in his private practice, I kept bugging him to hypnotize me, but one stern look from my father put an abrupt end to those requests. But, I must say, as a little kid, the most interesting cousin was Joe, who owned and operated a Carvel Ice Cream stand. That was a most enjoyable afternoon visit featuring a large banana split, both designed and eaten by yours truly!

However, my favorite Rhode Island cousin of all had to be Frank Fusco. Frank was a big man who was married to sweet cousin Julia. I believe Frank was in the construction business, but I couldn't really be sure. He drank his favorite homemade wine from early morning until late in the evening but somehow never got drunk. He looked like a cross between Santa Claus and Luca Brasi. When Frank hugged you, you disappeared until he decided to let go. He had a heart of gold, and to stay overnight at his home was an adventure. Julia loved to cook, and Frank made a tomato pie that was so good, you would think about it all the way back to Philly. Their home was equipped with an entire basement kitchen. Of course, they had one upstairs too, but the basement room was where most of the delicacies were created. The stairwell to the basement had a low overhang midway down, and whenever a visitor bumped his head, the next thing you'd hear was Frank bellowing, "Watch my head!"

We saw Frank and Julia more frequently in Philadelphia than in Warwick. Frank's business allowed him to have more freedom to travel than did my father's union factory job. However, after I graduated from college and worked as business manager of athletics at Temple University, I seized an opportunity to see Frank and Julia at their home. In the fall of 1970, Temple's football team traveled to Kingston to take on the University of Rhode Island in a Saturday afternoon contest. Since it was my job to set up all travel arrangements and related details, I naturally accompanied the team. Our hotel in Kingston was only a 35-minute drive to Warwick. I called Frank and Julia to tell them I'd be stopping over on that Friday night to visit. Of course, they "forced" me to come for dinner, and I jubilantly accepted the invitation.

Before hopping into my rented Chevy Impala, I toyed with the idea of bringing one of my co-workers along but decided against it so as not to impose on Julia. When I arrived at their house around 6:00 p.m., I was bear-hugged by Big Frank, kissed by them both, and led to the basement dinner table. Julia told me that I should have brought a friend with me. I made it downstairs safely, without bumping my head, despite Frank watching intently for the opportunity to deliver his famous line!

So this would be a meal for only three people.

As Frank poured the wine, Julia brought out the first course: a giant bowl of freshly gathered quahog clams on the half shell. Frank and his buddy had just dug them up that morning, and they were great served chilled with Julia's homemade cocktail sauce.

Next came a giant macaroni dish filled with homemade raviolis, accompanied by dishes of meatballs, sausage, and pork from the gravy. Naturally, this was served with crusty Italian bread, baked by Julia only hours before.

Next came the large dish of fried chicken, drumsticks and thighs - very crispy.

Next came the beautiful garden salad, with imported extra virgin olive oil and fresh wine vinegar made by Frank himself.

Finally, Julia's pineapple cheesecake, made with ricotta cheese, along with fresh-brewed espresso.

The meal could have easily fed 10 people.

It was after 10:00 before we finally got up from the table. I hugged them both and, shortly afterwards, headed back to the hotel. I was stuffed, but, at 23, I could recover quickly and actually felt pretty good on the ride back. The next day's game would start at 1:00 p.m., and Frank made me promise to stop by in the morning before I went to the stadium.

So, at 9:30 a.m., I pulled into their driveway, looking forward to giving them both one more hug and thanking them again for the wonderful meal and the love we shared. After doing so, I turned to leave the house, and Frank told me to wait. From the oven, he took out a whole, rectangular tomato pie, wrapped it in aluminum foil, and gave it to me to take home.

The tomato pie made it back to Buist Avenue in southwest Philly that night to be shared with Mom and Dad, with love, from Big Frank and Julia.

13

What's in a Name?

My "Uncle Jerry" in 1992

LOOKING BACK, IT must have been in the early '70s. I was still living at home in Philadelphia, and it was a long, hot summer. On top of that, there was a severe drought in Pennsylvania. The drought got so bad that KYW Radio decided, as a public service, to have an official from the Philadelphia Suburban Water Company - which was based in Bryn Mawr - come on the air to give daily updates and advice about coping with the situation. Now, these facts are interesting enough, given the rarity of the events, but they were doubly intriguing to me because the guy providing the radio updates was named Jerry Sacchetti, V.P. of Public Relations for the water company. He was quite thorough in presenting the bad news every day, but he still projected a friendly personality and an optimistic viewpoint. Once, he came on the air while I was listening with my father in the living room, and I asked Dad if Jerry was related to us. Dad gave a matter-of-fact, "No." Up to that point, I hadn't seen many people with our surname who weren't family, so I was even more intrigued. Who was this big shot, and where was he from? But I never found out; the drought eventually ended, and life went on.

About 10 years later, in 1983, I began my sales career. Being an outside, commission-only salesman of industrial chemicals, my job was to go out and convert non-customers into customers! That meant making a lot of "cold calls," which involved walking up to perfect strangers and using techniques I had learned to find the buyer, present and demonstrate my products, and close the sale. This is not an easy task and certainly not for the faint of heart or for one who takes rejection personally. My territory was Montgomery County, Pennsylvania. I lived in Drexel Hill at the time, and this area of responsibility reached as far west as Pottstown, some 30 miles away. Other towns in my territory included Norristown,

Limerick, Collegeville, and part of the Main Line area, which consisted of Lower Merion, Gladwyne, and - yes - Bryn Mawr.

When planning my next-day sales calls, I would ride into the area and list places I considered to be promising. One day, about six or eight months into my sales career, I was driving down Lancaster Avenue when I saw a nice building with a sign which read: Philadelphia Suburban Water Co. To me, this had some potential, since I noticed company trucks outside and a maintenance shop. I had several products that could be useful there, so I listed the water company as a stop for the next day. The following morning, as I pulled into the parking lot, I noticed a sign on the wall that read: Reserved Sacchetti. It all came flooding back to me from 10 years earlier, and I thought, *This must be for the guy I heard on the radio that summer.*

As I parked in the visitor spot, an idea hit me. It was a big gamble and could prove to be either a disaster or a bonanza. In sales, it is most important to get the opportunity to speak with the right people who can actually help you. The higher a person's rank in an organization, the more difficult it is to have an audience. Knowing this, I decided to take the plunge!

I entered the building and scanned the directory, which said that Jerry Sacchetti's office was in the executive suite on the top floor. I took the elevator and, when the door opened, saw a large, circular desk that accommodated three receptionists for the executives of the company. Please realize that receptionists are trained to ward off salespeople who just walk up to them and do not have appointments with the boss. I knew these ladies must be good at their job. For a moment,

I thought I saw notches carved in the desk representing each vanquished salesman! However, the attractive brunette that I approached with a smile was more than happy to assist me when I handed her my business card and said:

"I'd like to see my uncle Jerry, please."

She glanced at my card and replied, "Oh, certainly." By then my adrenal glands were on afterburners. She asked me to wait while she entered Jerry's office to announce me. His words rang out:

"Who the hell is this?"

I walked over to his doorway and exclaimed, "Uncle Jerry!"

He said, "Who the hell are you?"

I gave him a big smile, sat down opposite him, and related the whole story, from listening to him on the radio to my spontaneous idea to see him. He burst out laughing and congratulated me on getting in to meet him. We spoke for about an hour, first cross-checking to see if we were related, then talking about how he was a musician, then about my baseball career. It was great; *he* was great.

By the time we were through, he had provided me with names of people I should see in the company, at different locations - all potential buyers. I had absolutely no trouble regarding my initial contacts, since Jerry had given me permission to say that he sent me, and I used that tactic to the fullest. (They all got my business card, too!) Suffice it to say that I started doing business with multiple locations. In 2004, the company became a division of Aqua America.

Sometimes hunches pay off, and even a drought can become a steady stream. Jerry passed away in 2006; may he rest in peace. Thanks to his gracious willingness to help a struggling salesman who took a chance, that company and I are still doing business today.

14

Checking In

The author's first car phone

IN MARCH OF 2019, I had a follow-up appointment with my Cooper Hospital orthopedic surgeon, who had repaired my three ruptured quadriceps tendons exactly one year before. While in the waiting room, I saw eight other patients. One was sleeping, one was admiring the ceiling, and the remaining six were playing on their smartphones. As I put my semi-intelligent phone down on the empty seat next to me, I thought about the time when I had to regularly "check in" and how this tool, which we now take for granted, would have been a Godsend.

As an outside salesman since 1983, I had no employer-provided office, so it was my responsibility to contact our headquarters daily at midday and late in the afternoon. This was necessary because the only way my customers could reach me to place an order or for assistance was to call our main number. They would leave a message, and I would respond as quickly as possible. This deceptively simple process had a variety of pitfalls.

First of all, it was a miracle if you found a payphone that actually worked, since some parts of my territory were in high-crime areas, and vandals considered payphones precursors to ATM machines. A screwdriver used just so was excellent for relieving the phone of its contents. On the rare occasion that you found one with an actual dial tone, you'd have to first check the mouthpiece. Kids liked to unscrew the bottom of the receiver and remove the amplifier, making it impossible to be heard on the other end. After getting burned a few times and realizing I was talking to myself, I started the self-check procedure on a regular basis.

Even if the payphone was in working condition, amplifier and all, there was a better-than-even chance that it was a haven for nearly every germ known to man. So you didn't dare put the phone to your ear if you happened to see evidence of foreign matter on the receiver. Then, of course, there was the possibility of the phone simply malfunctioning. I am not proud of it, but, in a fit of rage, I was known to bang a receiver or two onto the top of the phone after a very important call was dropped in the middle of a rainstorm. I must say, however, that even though my primal display made me feel a little better, the payphone still didn't work, and I never got my quarters back! Live and learn.

But, in life, every torment eventually ends or at least becomes a bit more tolerable. For me, this occurred when some genius at the phone company invented payphones that were to be installed about three or four feet off the ground. When I first saw one at a gas station in West Conshohocken, Pennsylvania, I thought that it was custom-made and installed in case Danny DeVito came to town. However, upon further observation, I realized it was designed so that drivers of automobiles could pull up to the phone and lean out of the window to make a call. To me, this invention ranked right up there with the wheel. No more standing in the rain or snow. No, sir, I could sit in the car, in relative comfort, and still make my calls. Additionally, since these modern marvels were usually installed in high-visibility areas, there was little chance that they would be vandalized or otherwise abused. The phone company had developed a great product - one that would obviously earn revenue with low cost of vandalism repairs. Win for them; win for me. But there was even better news to come.

In 1991, something happened to me that made even the "DeVito" payphone seem so-so. My company held one of its exciting sales contests. If a salesperson met the criteria, you would be awarded a revolutionary, state-of-the-art prize guaranteed to change the world as we knew it. And that it did. You see, the contest winners were given a Panasonic EB-2501 car phone. Although big and bulky by today's standards, to me winning that phone was like hitting the lottery. What an amazing tool it would be! No longer would I have to endure weather, filth, germs, lost quarters, or crazy people coming up to me asking for money while I stood at the payphone. I had hit the big leagues.

I gratefully accepted my carphone at one of our sales meetings on a Saturday in July. The first call I made with it was to my wife, just after crossing the Tacony-Palmyra Bridge into New Jersey and spending 20 minutes figuring out how the thing worked. But it was my second call that I *really* looked forward to.

The very next day, I went to see my parents in southwest Philly. At the time, Mom and Dad were both in their 80s. I parked my car right in front of their Buist Avenue home and dialed their number. Mom answered the phone in the living room, which was situated near the picture window that faced the street. I told Mom that I planned to stop by later to pay them a visit. After she acknowledged my intention, I asked her to look out of the front window.

"What are you talking about, Charlie?"

"Just look, Ma."

When she saw me on the phone in the car, her eyes opened wide in surprise and disbelief. My father abandoned his easy chair, looked at me, and gestured in a way that is best described as a warm, Italian greeting. It was a moment I never forgot. Sitting in the doctor's office decades later, watching those six strangers play with their devices, I thought of that day and wondered if their first cell phone ever provided such a simple but cherished memory.

15

Honey, I Told You So

Auto-repair shop destroyed by Floyd (Ossining, NY)

IN SEPTEMBER OF 1999, I did something very dumb. Not that it was the first time, mind you. For example, when I was 21, I bought an Alfa Romeo for the low, low price of $500, disregarding my father's advice. It was a mechanic's nightmare, became the symbol of non-locomotion on our block, and sat for so long that small trees began to grow under it. That was pretty dumb - however, it pales in comparison to that fall afternoon when I tried to outrun a hurricane.

At the time, I was a district sales manager for my company and scheduled to work with my salesman, Jeff La Fleur, in Westchester County, New York. He was a very good salesman but struggling a bit, so I planned to spend two days helping him refine his sales techniques as we worked his territory. As usual, I would be lodging at the Peekskill Inn in the beautiful Hudson Valley. On the morning of September 16th, Hurricane Floyd made landfall at Cape Fear, North Carolina, as a category-two hurricane, having weakened from its former near category-five status while it tore through the Bahamas. Although heavy rain was in the forecast for our area, it was only partly cloudy and warm in New Jersey. The weatherman said the storm was moving slowly, about 10 miles per hour, so I reasoned that I could hop on the turnpike, scoot up the Palisades Parkway, and zip into Peekskill before the rain hit, if indeed it rained at all. *Heck, the storm might not even come directly up the coast,* I thought, *so maybe I should take the calculated risk and get on the road.*

My wife, LuAnn, said, "Don't go. You must be nuts."

By then we had been married for 24 years, so I expect she knew, deep down in her precious heart, that I had a bit of a stubborn streak and generally did what I wanted once I made up my mind. Given all the facts - a weakening storm, my man needing help, the storm moving at 10 miles per hour while I would be driving at 70 - I decided to get going around 3:00 p.m. Unfortunately, there was one thing I didn't take into account: Hurricane Floyd was 1,000 miles wide, so it wouldn't be long before its effects would be felt in our area. With the New Jersey sky becoming gradually more ominous, I jumped into my Chrysler Concorde, wearing what I usually do when

I drive for a few hours in warm weather: t-shirt, shorts, and flip flops.

I was on the road for about 45 minutes when the rain began to fall pretty hard on the New Jersey Turnpike, but it wasn't too bad. When I got to the end of the turnpike and headed for the Palisades Parkway, the rain and wind were so intense that I began to strongly question my own intellectual capacity. By the time I entered the elevated parkway and headed north, with the Hudson River in the valley below, I was convinced that I was an idiot.

The parkway is cut through a line of massive cliffs called the Palisades. Springs were gushing through the hills, and the water cascaded onto the paved parkway, which collected the water like a giant basin. All traffic was at a standstill. As I squinted through my car window, I saw the water rising to mid-tire height. I started to look for a tree to climb or at least a low-hanging branch to cling to. As a non-swimmer, I was in trouble, and I firmly believed the rushing water would wash all of the cars down the embankment. Even though the time was about 5:00 p.m., it was pitch dark, with the vehicle lights providing the only illumination. My cell phone didn't work. The wind gusts were powerful enough to shake the car. I offered more than a few prayers, realizing this might be *it* for me.

I thought of the admonition, "Don't go. You must be nuts."

That was the first time I experienced feeling completely helpless.

But then an angel appeared in the form of a New York state cop in an SUV, driving half on the road and half on the median strip. With lights flashing and sirens blaring, he worked his way to the jammed cars and led us up onto the strip, escorting us single file through the wooded section to the opposite, less-traveled southbound lanes, and finally to an exit.

I was safe.

Shaken but relieved, I carefully drove past numerous fallen trees and around flooded streets. There was no power, so it was completely dark. My cell phone finally worked, so I called home to let everyone know I was safe. There were no vacancies at any nearby hotels, and I was still about 25 miles away from the Peekskill Inn. I ended up sleeping in my car in the parking lot of the Tarrytown, New York, Holiday Inn. The blanket I always kept in the trunk finally came in handy. At 5:00 a.m. I left the parking lot and eventually arrived at my hotel in Peekskill. Jeff and I were able to get in the two days of work I had planned. They were as productive as possible, given that there was widespread flooding, and the area was littered with abandoned cars and fallen trees.

When I arrived home, there were hugs and kisses all around, from my wife and two kids. Soon after, I figured I might as well face the music, so I turned to LuAnn and admitted, "You were right, Sweetie."

Her expression said: What else is new?

16

An Ounce of Pandemonium

Thanks for "dropping in"

I AM ALWAYS amazed by the way many people react when they encounter some of nature's smallest and weakest creatures. Watching a burly, macho man jump, scream, or bolt at the sight of a mouse or an insect really cracks me up. Why the panic; why the fear? If we think logically about such an encounter, we must concede that it's extremely unlikely that a mouse that runs by us will drag us off for lunch. Bumblebees really aren't interested in attacking people; they just want the pollen. No need to run for cover (unless you're allergic) if one of them buzzes by on its way to a floral banquet. Still, overreacting happens, and such reactions, in a variety of situations, have provided me with more than a few laughs over the years.

Once, when I was in high school, my buddy invited me to Sunday dinner. His family's home had a connecting door to the next house in the row, which was occupied by his grandfather, his mom's sister, and her family. The sisters were very close, so it was not unusual for them to share a meal. What *was* a tad unusual was dessert that day. After enjoying a delicious roast beef dinner, out came the homemade chocolate cake, along with a box of freshly-made doughnuts from a place called Donut Land, just outside of the Philadelphia city limits.

As we were about to enjoy the pastries, my buddy's aunt reached over to grab one of her favorite vanilla-cream doughnuts, with the white powdered-sugar coating. After sipping her freshly brewed Maxwell House, she calmly lifted her treat and broke it in half so she could bite into it without getting powder all over her face. As she glanced at the inside of the pastry, she made direct eye contact with a cream-filled roach, who wasn't quite dead and obviously enjoying his last few moments. Her scream made the crystal chandelier shake. The other adults gasped. My buddy and I laughed, as you might expect of two knuckle-headed teens.

When the smoke cleared, we enjoyed the chocolate cake. Hold the doughnuts!

Then there was the time when my wife, LuAnn, and I were

newlyweds, and we decided to eat lunch at a local Burger King in Drexel Hill, Pennsylvania. The place was clean and very well kept, despite what is often expected from a fast food joint. As a real stickler for cleanliness, my wife appreciated this, as well as the various floral arrangements neatly set in rectangular boxes on counter-like surfaces around the restaurant. After picking up our Whoppers, fries, and Cokes, we chose a particularly attractive table next to one of the counters topped with a flower box. As we took our seats, it wasn't our intention to disturb anyone - or anything - but apparently we did. A little gray mouse streaked along the counter top and suddenly leaped into the flower box as though jumping into bed for its afternoon nap. With an abrupt shriek, LuAnn deserted her Whopper and bolted for the door. I took mine with me and enjoyed it at home. We lived in that neighborhood for 10 years, but LuAnn never visited that Burger King again. I, on the other hand, was more forgiving.

These experiences can't compare with one that occurred in Indianapolis in 2003. My company had purchased a new computer program meant to revolutionize how we tracked customer contacts, purchases, and sales figures. So the boss had all of the sales staff meet at our Indianapolis office for two days of training with the program developers. At the end of the second day, which was a Friday evening, we all headed to a very fancy restaurant downtown. This place was really something to behold. It was designed with an outdoor motif and filled - or should I say "stuffed"? - with taxidermied animals like deer, antelope, and birds of prey; and they were all displayed in natural settings. You felt as though you were enjoying a gourmet meal in the middle of the woods, with all of the beauty but none of the pitfalls. The menu included a wide variety of meat dishes, including elk and venison, along with an ample supply of non-game meats.

Our party of about 20 sat in a prime location with several animals nearby, including a stuffed bobcat perched directly above us in a tree. Another nice touch was the fact that we were seated next to a party of 12, celebrating the 95th birthday of their sweet grandmother. We all chatted freely with one another as we waited for our food, and they were very cordial, making us feel right at home. After we consumed more than a few adult beverages, our food arrived, and we dug in. The meal was great. Granny's group had simultaneously received their orders, and everyone was happy. About 10 minutes later, we were startled by the screams of all of the women at Granny's table.

It seems an unstuffed - *live* - and very clumsy mouse had lost its footing, plummeting from the tree above, plunging head-first into Granny's dish of beef medallions!

Pandemonium erupted. The table was overturned. Food was flying all over the place. Other guests started screaming, as did a few waitresses. After the initial shock, most of our group dissolved into uncontrollable laughter. Two managers ran over in an attempt to quell the chaos. The scene was reminiscent of a Marx Brothers movie. The head manager did his best to gain control and said there would be no charge for their meals - even going so far as to offer them a new table and fresh food, mice not included!. It all was refused; Granny and company made a beeline for the exit. We, however, settled down to finish what turned out to be a delightful meal.

I don't know what happened to that little mouse after its free-fall into Granny's dish, but I know he gave a bunch of people a night to remember.

17

Fun in Acapulco?

Author applying rust converter on an Acapulco rooftop

IT WAS HOT in Acapulco, Mexico, in February of 2004. Unfortunately, I wasn't there to enjoy the sunshine and the warm tropical ocean; I was there to work because the specialty chemical company that I represented had decided to expand their reach south of the border. We found an opportunity through an agent who facilitated our meetings with Telmex, the largest telecommunications company in the region. The powers that be decided our best shot to earn the business was to demonstrate one of our most unique products, a rust neutralizer that stopped existing rust in its tracks. Telmex had numerous structures, and its Acapulco site would be the toughest test because of the ocean environment and humid conditions. So I was tapped as the one to meet with our potential customer and actually apply the product. After it was applied, we would monitor the results for several months and, if all went well, start doing business.

My plane would land in Mexico City, where I would stay at a hotel and, the next day, attend several meetings. The following day, I would be driven to Acapulco for the demo. I was amazed at the condition of the freeway from Mexico City to Acapulco; it was in great shape, clean, and well lit. We would stay overnight in the resort town, at the Las Brisas Hotel, do the demo the next afternoon, and then drive back to Mexico City. The Las Brisas was famous as the favorite hotel of Frank Sinatra and his buddies. Every room had its own outdoor pool, and I remembered the lyrics of "Come Fly with Me," in which Ol' Blue Eyes mentions "beat[ing] the birds down to Acapulco bay." I could only imagine what those colorful characters did while staying there. If only the walls could talk!

The next day, we went up to the eighth-floor roof of a Telmex-owned facility to apply Stop Rust, our rust-neutralizing product, to several of its metal structures. It was 95°F on that February day, and my New Jersey body had a lot of acclimating to do, moving from the icebox to the oven in two days. All went well, and then it was time to begin the four-hour ride back to Mexico City. My Mexican companions invited me to pick a place for dinner. Prior to getting on the highway, I noticed a restaurant which looked interesting, so I asked to go there. The food was great! One of the dishes I enjoyed most was the tortilla chips, baked on site and served with various salsas. One of the salsas was green, and I was warned to be careful, as it was reputed to be very unfriendly to one's digestive system. As I tasted it, I noticed it wasn't even hot. I scoffed good-naturedly at my Mexican buddies, telling them it wasn't that spicy, and, besides, I could handle spicy foods pretty well. I continued to enjoy the mysterious green salsa throughout the meal.

They just looked at me and smiled. So did the waiter, but he also gave me a Mexican chuckle.

After the delicious dinner, we drove onto the highway and sped away. About two hours into the trip, I felt a strange feeling in my belly. It wasn't painful, but I quickly realized it had the potential to make the final two hours of the drive a little too exciting. By that time, the guys were laughing and conversing in Spanish. I, on the other hand, found nothing to be amused about, and - after an hour - I urgently suggested a visit to the next rest stop. We did so, and I quickly made my way past the heavily armed military guard toward the men's room. I had heard that soldiers guarded public areas because of the drug trafficking, so I wasn't surprised to see him, but it didn't matter, anyway. He would have needed a cannon to stop me from getting to my destination at that moment. Ultimately, we visited three more rest stops along the way back to the hotel.

Throughout that night, I had no sleep but lots of exercise consisting of quick sprints from one room to another. I was worried that I wouldn't be able to make it to the airport for my 6:00 a.m. flight, but somehow I did. The flight was an adventure, and - I must admit - I violated the "fasten seat belt" sign a few times as I scurried hastily to the tiny restroom at the rear of the plane.

I learned a few things on that trip. First, I learned that Acapulco can be surprisingly hot in February. I also learned that our product would really benefit our customer in that humid environment. Last but not least, I learned, if you don't know the territory, it's best to listen to the locals!

18

Ol' Blue Eyes, Sid, and the Mother's Day Gift

Frank Sinatra

IN THE U.S., Mother's Day is celebrated on the second Sunday of May. Each time that special day arrives, I can't help but think of a particular one that I'll never forget, but the story actually starts two weeks before Mother's Day in 2002. It was a beautiful, sunny Friday, and I decided to visit my customer, John Hughes, who was the facilities manager at Temple University's Ambler, Pennsylvania, campus. I always enjoyed my interactions with John, my friend for many years and a great guy to be with. Aside from doing business, a trip to Ambler was a treat because of the beautiful flowers and trees that adorned the grounds. The campus on that day, April 26th, displayed God's splendor in all directions. When I finished my sales visit, I hopped into my car and decided to call my elderly parents, Henry and Kate, to see how they were. It was about lunch time, and I knew they would be home from Mom's weekly visit to her hairdresser. Although both in their 90s, they were fiercely independent, and Dad provided transportation to and from Mom's appointment, since she never learned to drive. That phone call is forever etched in my mind.

When Dad answered, I heard bewilderment in his voice - certainly out of character for the tough guy who taught me how to be a man. While he was outside in front of the house, checking his flower garden, Mom was inside making his lunch. When he came in and didn't see her in the kitchen, he rushed forward and found her lying on the floor - Mom had suffered a stroke. I told him to call 911, which he did. As I sped to the University of Pennsylvania Hospital, my mind was racing. Since Mom had arrived at the hospital relatively quickly after the onset of the stroke, we were told that surgery would give her a 50-50 chance of survival. We consented to the operation.

Mom lasted two weeks, never regaining consciousness, and passed away peacefully on May 11th, the day before Mother's Day. When I received that late-night call, there was an air of peace. Mom was deeply religious and certainly had no fear of dying. I decided to wait until morning to tell my father. Dad had held out hope and always believed that Mom would survive, even after we all agreed that no further extraordinary measures would be taken, just to keep her "alive." When I told Dad that Mom had passed away, he shared that when the EMT's lifted Mom onto the gurney to take her to the hospital, she told them she had to finish making Dad's lunch first! He smiled when he told me, not surprised that as she had done for 65 years, Mom would put him first no matter how dire the circumstances.

The next morning, I was home on Mother's Day, thinking about what had happened over the wondrous two weeks the family had shared with Mom at her bedside. I decided to go out and sit near my newly planted vegetable garden to clear my head while tuning in to Sid Mark's weekly radio broadcast, *Sunday with Sinatra*. As I listened to Frank's flawless crooning, I recalled how Mom was always proud of her youthful outlook on life. Even at her advanced age, she loved to have fun and always insisted that she wasn't old; she was "Young at Heart." I instantly felt the urge to hear that particular Sinatra song, both as a tribute to Mom and to give me some sort of closure.

I went into my house to call the radio station. I actually reached someone connected with the show, perhaps a producer, to whom I explained that my mother had just died, and it would be very kind of them - and a real blessing to me - if Sid played "Young at Heart." The man was very sympathetic but said that since the audience was so large, and they didn't want to disappoint all the people who couldn't get through, the decision was made early on not to accept any requests. I understood the policy but simply asked him to please mention my request to Sid anyway, just in case he would be gracious enough to make an exception. Promising nothing, the man gave me his sincere condolences, and we ended our conversation.

I returned to my folding chair on that beautiful Mother's Day morning and took a deep breath of the cool, crisp air that brought me both peace and calm. As I watched two small rabbits playing "tag" under my cherry tree, my attention was drawn back to my little radio. Hearing nothing else in the little piece of heaven I call my backyard, an unmistakable sound emerged over the airwaves:

"Fairy tales can come true; it can happen to you, if you're young at heart ..."

I looked up at the powder-blue sky, and - as the tears rolled down my cheeks - I wished Mom a happy Mother's Day.

19

The Temperamental Discovery

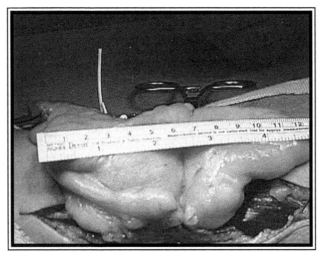

Post-surgery photo

ON A FRIDAY afternoon late in February of 2007, I was fully engrossed in composing a lengthy proposal to present to my customer in a few days. The document contained my recommendations and reasons why I felt a particular floor coating would best suit his needs. I also included application instructions along with a cost analysis. My two-hour investment was well spent, as I thought the proposal was very good. All I had to do was finish typing it, meet with him on Wednesday, and close the sale.

And then it happened: My computer froze. For half an hour, my every attempt to "awaken" it failed. I tried calling my computer-savvy buddy but couldn't reach him. I am not blessed with an abundance of patience, so what little I had left was soon to be history. I tried one more thing, which only finished it off.

Gone - *poof* - deleted.

All of my work was for naught, since I hadn't yet backed it up. At that moment, I did the only thing that made sense to me as an emotional Italian/Sicilian-American: I yelled out an expletive and banged my right fist onto the top of my computer desk. I felt pretty foolish for failing to back up my work, but I felt even more so when I glanced at my right forearm and saw how badly it was swollen. I remember thinking to myself, "You idiot. You not only lost your work, but you probably broke a bone in your forearm. What a moron!" To make matters worse, my daughter Rosie and I were looking forward to our Phillies spring training trip to Clearwater, Florida, in just a few short weeks. I could picture myself basking in the hot sun behind home plate, sporting a fashionable forearm cast.

Surprisingly, though, I felt no pain. I called my doctor, who asked me to come right over. She took one look at my forearm and ordered an x-ray, which showed no broken bones. That softened the blow a bit. She told me that it should get better in a week or so and to ice it for 24 hours. The weekend was uneventful; still no pain, but my arm remained swollen.

Rosie and I went to spring training and had a great time. The arm didn't bother me at all. Still, I was concerned when, after four weeks, the swelling hadn't decreased. When I arrived home, I decided to get checked out by my orthopedist. He looked at the x-ray and concurred that there was no break, saying that the swelling should go down eventually. When mid-May rolled around with no change, I knew that we were missing something, so I went back to my orthopedist. At that point he seemed concerned and ordered an MRI, but nothing on the MRI troubled him, orthopedically speaking. The next move was for me to get evaluated by a hand surgeon, so in late May I went to see a well-renowned surgeon in the area.

When the surgeon and I sat down in the exam room, he took one look at the MRI images and uttered, "You have a tumor in your forearm." My reaction was quick and to the point: "Let's get it the hell out of there." He asked me when I could be ready for surgery, and I said, "Tomorrow." That didn't exactly work for him, so we set it up for June 12th, roughly two weeks later. All of the pre-op things were done, and I had to return to the office for a pre-surgery session. I was very impressed when he took at least ten measurements of my hand and forearm, from every angle, every which way. He explained that the tumor was probably a benign lipoma, but it still could do some nerve damage due to its size and proximity. In fact, my right hand was a bit numb, but I hadn't thought much of it until his comment.

On June 12th, I went to the surgical center in Voorhees, New Jersey, and the doctor did his magic, removing the tumor. At the post-surgery visit, he described it as the "largest lipoma of its type" that he had ever seen. I thanked God that it was a lipoma and therefore benign. And I always thought I had big forearms because I was strong!

When I first awoke in the recovery room - drowsy and hungry - I saw my wife, LuAnn, and then glanced at two nurses, who were nervously giggling at a piece of paper they were studying that appeared to be a photo. The image showed the lipoma just after removal. A six-inch ruler was behind it to provide scale. When the nurses showed it to me in my semi-conscious state, I took one look at it and asked, "Did Frank Perdue assist in the operation?" because the tumor resembled a chicken breast. They laughed and agreed, but LuAnn wouldn't look at it. Characteristically, I promptly asked for something to eat.

I am grateful to say that I recovered well, despite a little residual numbness in my hand. I also have an impressive six-inch surgical scar, so if I ever decide to rob a bank, I'll be sure not to do it in a t-shirt! What was funny about this whole episode was that the tumor had taken 60 years to reach that size, and I had never noticed my enlarged forearm. I probably never would have had I not lost my temper and smashed the desk with my fist.

Sometimes Italian/Sicilian genes can be a blessing!

20

A Stinging Defeat

Young Kenny shows his style

FALL HAS ALWAYS been my favorite time of the year. I find the crisp air, the array of colors, and the bright skies of autumn both lovely and invigorating. Additionally, since 2013, I have another reason to look forward to this time of year because October of 2013 was the first time that my friend Bill Winarski and I attended the annual Al Pisa Memorial Bocce Tournament held at the Pisa residence in the Bunker Hill section of Dunmore, Pennsylvania. We continue to enjoy annual attendance each October. As I explained in my story "When an Impulse pays off," which appears in my earlier book, *It's All Good: Times and Events I'd Never Want to Change*, a chance phone call I made in 2012 led me to enjoy a wonderful friendship with Al's closest friends and family, especially his son, Carlo, and Carlo's son, Alfredo. Carlo faithfully continues this bocce tournament, a tradition of love and friendship that Al started many years ago.

Al's vision was to host this annual get-together at his home, which meant he would do almost all of the cooking and preparation. Of course, the guests rarely come empty-handed, usually bringing Italian specialties such as roasted peppers, eggplant marinated in olive oil and spices, pepperoni, sharp provolone, wine, and crusty Italian bread. All of these, however, are merely pre-meal snacks to be enjoyed with beverages under Carlo's large grapevine. The real dinner begins after the bocce tournament. This feast is where our host shines as the provider of various pasta dishes, meatballs, hot and sweet sausage, chicken, salad, and whatever else he deems fit for the occasion. Dessert is the specialty of one of the guests, Dave "The Mailman" Evanko, a master baker who prepares the most creative and delicious pastries imaginable.

And then there is the bocce tournament! It's important to note that I use the term "tournament" in its loosest form. There is very little structure. No officials or judges preside, and sometimes a half hour may pass between games as the competing pairs fuel up on Chianti or Merlot. Rules are loosely followed, probably because no one really knows what they are. When someone makes a good shot, everybody yells. When a guy makes a bad shot, everybody gives him the business. It's all about fun and camaraderie. The first year that we attended, we were dubbed "The Jersey Boys." Bill and I had never played bocce in our lives, but we won the tournament, primarily because we made a couple of lucky shots, bouncing the wooden ball off of the railroad ties which still serve as court borders. No skill was necessary. In October of 2014, we chose to make a grand entrance, carrying jugs of wine and reminding all of our buddies that we were the defending champs. We lost miserably, barely winning one game out of the six we played. Our cockiness soon faded. In 2015 and 2016, we gave similar performances as we, and every other team, fell victim to a bona fide bocce star.

In 2015, Ken Gaughan, one of the guys and a yearly attendee, brought along his 15-year-old son, Kenny Jr., to the festivities. As partners, they crushed all their opponents. Pop was good, but Kenny was *amazing*. Almost every shot he took came within inches of the *pallina*, a small ball that is the target at which you shoot. The closer your larger ball gets to it, the higher your score. Kenny was untouchable that day. He and his dad whipped everyone again in 2016, but he was such a nice kid that I found myself rooting for him. Not the least bit arrogant, Kenny just annihilated all opponents.

But fate would pay a visit to the Pisa bocce court in 2017.

That year, Bill and I actually played well and defeated three teams. Kenny and Ken were still alive, and - as luck would have it - we would face them in the final game of 21 points. I was rolling against Kenny; Bill was to take on his dad. With the score tied at 18, the match-deciding game came down to Kenny's final throw. If he put his shot inside of mine, they would win their third consecutive championship. If not, the bragging rights would again belong to the Jersey Boys. As 25 guys watched, Kenny intently studied the court. He saw a path to victory if he could roll the ball between three others. Having seen Kenny easily make that shot many times, I was certain he'd do it again. As Kenny took a step and swung his arm back to release the ball, he was stung by a bee right on his hand. The pain of the sting forced him to release the ball prematurely, so it traveled only a few feet.

Game over. The Jersey Boys were back!

After shaking hands (gently) with Kenny and his dad, Bill and I retired to the grapevine and treated ourselves to a few pieces of provolone and pepperoni. That was where we started the rumor that we had brought the bee with us from Jersey to be tactically released at the most critical moment.

I think most of the guys believed we were kidding, but it's never too early to start playing head games on your opponents at the Al Pisa Memorial Bocce Tournament.

21

A Friend and a Hero

Joe Sr. and Nora with sons
(from left) Kevin, Joe Jr., Jim, Sean, and Dan

IF YOU HAD seen Joe Smith back in the '50s and early '60s, envisioning a "Philadelphia hero" wouldn't have been your first thought. "Smitty" was a great pal with a good sense of humor who could never be confused with a weightlifter. Although a thin, quiet guy, he certainly was a hard worker, diligently maintaining his year-round portable Sunday news-paper stand outside of St. Barnabas Church on 63rd and Buist Avenue. There, he would set up stacks of the Sunday *Inquirer* and the rival Sunday *Bulletin* for sale to parishioners exiting the Masses from 6:00 a.m. until after noon. I remember him scurrying to keep the papers intact when the weather got nasty. He accomplished this by covering them up with plastic and using whatever he could find to keep the covers from blowing away. Aside from the weather battles, his other major challenge was to keep his sanity while dealing with the incessant yapping of eight or so Chihuahuas owned by the pastor, Father Joseph LaRue, as they ran up and down the adjacent yard, asserting their territorial rights.

At West Catholic High School, Smitty became quite a cross-country runner - good enough to earn a scholarship to Temple University. It was during those years that I was privileged to get to know him better. As a baseball player and fellow athlete at Temple, I shared the comradery with Smitty which developed while competing for the glory of the same school. We swapped stories about our respective coaches, both of them real characters. We also shared something else: a number of road trips, each lasting 45 minutes to an hour, from home to school in his old Chevy Nova. Smitty had one of those "state-of-the-art" 8-track tape players in his car. Kids today may laugh at that description, but, back in the '60s, that was quite a leap in technology. He used to listen to that tape player every day. The problem was that he only had one tape that worked: The Supremes' *Greatest Hits*. Poor Diana Ross certainly earned her money in that car.

I remember one hot sunny day when the tape finally had it, and

Diana sounded like a foghorn on one of the Delaware River tugboats that we could hear from our southwest Philly homes. When I said, "Smitty, I think it's time to get rid of this tape," his reply was, "No, it's just the heat; the tape is dragging." I told him that the tape seemed ready to self-destruct like the ones on *Mission Impossible*. Joe loved those Supremes, and he wasn't giving up that easily.

The strength of his positive attitude was lost on me then but would soon be revealed.

While at Temple, Smitty enrolled in the Reserve Officer Training Corps, better known as ROTC. Students who completed this program would earn an officer's commission upon graduation. Back then, that meant a better-than-likely chance that you would be sent to Vietnam to play soldier for real, which was why most students wouldn't go anywhere near that program. Smitty embraced it. Not surprisingly, upon graduation in 1968, Smitty earned his commission as a second lieutenant and would eventually be sent to Vietnam to serve as an armored cavalry platoon leader. His platoon's job was to protect the nearby highway and bridges, removing any landmines planted by the enemy. This would help ensure safe passage for the good guys, who were constantly dealing with multiple threats.

As with all of our brave soldiers, Joe experienced quite a culture shock in Vietnam. This nice kid from the neighborhood, who ran cross-country and sold newspapers outside of church, saw his first fatality on his *first* day "in country" when a GI's weapon discharged by mistake. Soon after, he was wounded himself when the two-story tower in which he was quartered was hit by a rocket and collapsed onto him as he slept on the bottom floor. Cut and bleeding above the eye, he was stitched up and back with the men he led by afternoon. Our buddy had earned a Purple Heart.

Following Smitty's tour and upon his discharge from the Army, it was time to get back to civilian life. After the hell of war, you might expect him to seek a quiet office job, free of stress and danger, right?

Wrong!

Joe Smith became a Philadelphia cop in August of 1971. He served the city for 23 years, working the mean streets of some of its most dangerous districts, such as 55th and Pine (nick-named 55th and "Crime") and the 16th district at 39th and Lancaster Avenue. He retired from the police department in April of 1994. By then Smitty had married his lovely wife, Nora, and then there were the boys. By the time they were done, five wonderful sons blessed their household. So let's sum up: Joe had fought in a war, worked a dangerous job for 23 years as a Philly cop and, thank God, had earned a pension. Maybe now he could find a nice, easy job for a change, so he could coast a bit while raising those boys.

Not quite!

Joe Smith became Officer Joe Smith of the St. Joseph's University Campus security department, where he could use all of the knowledge gained from his wealth of experience to both perform and supervise at a very high level. Joe's sense of responsibility continued to motivate him. He knew that those boys would need an education to go out into the world and be successful. He also knew that aside from being a great place to work for many reasons, St. Joe's also offered a tuition-remission program which allowed children of full-time employees to attend that wonderful school for free! Joe Smith's career at St. Joe's University lasted from 1994 to 2017, 23 years. Although he could have retired, he kept working until age 70 just to make sure his boys were educated.

Now all five of Joe and Nora's sons have college degrees.

The skinny paperboy who fought off the wind and tolerated the crazy Chihuahuas grew up to be a man that served God; his country; his city; and, of course, his family.

Heroes never take the easy way out.

22

Giving Your Heart

Our little guy at age two

BY NO MEANS would I call myself a lover of poets or poetry. In my freshman poetry course at Temple University, I struggled greatly in my effort to understand guys like James Joyce, E. E. Cummings, and John Keats. To boot, my professor was one of those "way out" fellows who had a striking resemblance to Maynard G. Krebs, along with a very similar demeanor. I could barely understand *him*! Taken altogether, you can see how the course was not a favorite of this baseball-playing accounting major. As the years went by, my lack of interest in any poem persisted until I heard talk-show host Bill Bennett give an emotionally charged reading of Rudyard Kipling's "The Power of the Dog" on the day that Bennett's pet died. As I recall, it was about 2005. It struck me then and even more so in 2015, when we had to put our pet Yorkie to sleep at the age of 16.

The Power of the Dog
Rudyard Kipling (1865-1936)

There is sorrow enough in the natural way
From men and women to fill our day;
And when we are certain of sorrow in store,
Why do we always arrange for more?
Brothers and Sisters, I bid you beware
Of giving your heart to a dog to tear.

Buy a pup and your money will buy
Love unflinching that cannot lie—
Perfect passion and worship fed
By a kick in the ribs or a pat on the head.
Nevertheless it is hardly fair
To risk your heart for a dog to tear.

When the fourteen years which Nature permits
Are closing in asthma, or tumour, or fits,
And the vet's unspoken prescription runs
To lethal chambers or loaded guns,
Then you will find—it's your own affair—
But… you've given your heart to a dog to tear.

When the body that lived at your single will,
With its whimper of welcome, is stilled (how still!).
When the spirit that answered your every mood

Is gone—wherever it goes—for good,
You will discover how much you care,
And will give your heart to a dog to tear.

We've sorrow enough in the natural way,
When it comes to burying Christian clay.
Our loves are not given, but only lent,
At compound interest of cent per cent.
Though it is not always the case, I believe,
That the longer we've kept 'em, the more do we grieve:
For, when debts are payable, right or wrong,
A short-time loan is as bad as a long—
So why in—Heaven (before we are there)
Should we give our hearts to a dog to tear?

In 1999 my wife, LuAnn, and I decided that Rosie, our daughter, deserved a reward for several reasons. She had fought tenaciously to emerge victorious in a multi-year legal battle against our town's board of education and had been of enormous help to our family, assuming extra duties as her mother embarked on the student-teaching phase of her advanced degree in education. Rosie wanted a Yorkshire terrier, so I went to work to find a suitable breeder. I have always believed that the best way to find a good recommendation for something you need is to "pick the brains" of those you respect and whose advice you hold in high esteem. A customer of mine told me about a lady in Reading, Pennsylvania, who bred Yorkies at home in a loving, family atmosphere. So we followed his suggestion in November and traveled 75 miles to the home of the breeder - a young mother with her two-year-old in her arms - and checked out the pups. Only two Yorkies were left from the litter of eight: a male and a female. Rosie picked up the male, and he greeted her in a very special way: He licked her face and peed on her coat. How can you turn down such a creative pup? Rosie had found her Yorkie.

As time went by, we experienced the wonderful blessing of a pet who simply brightened our day and made us happy. Our pup was both paper trained in and raised in a crate, and he took to doing his business there very easily. Whenever he needed to, he would run into his cage and go on the newspaper. Of course, an enthusiastic, "Good boy," and a treat followed each visit to his *Philadelphia Inquirer* restroom. One day, I was working at my computer, lining up tomorrow's sales calls. I was analyzing my customer account cards, which measured 8.5" x 11", and they were on the floor next to my chair. The pup scampered into my office to say hello, and I paused momentarily to pick him up and pet him. To show his appreciation for my greeting, he proceeded to relieve himself on my account cards, no doubt noting that they were indeed made of paper and therefore "fair game." What could I do? I said, "Good boy," and gave him a treat. After all, I had plenty of blank account cards, and he had done just as he was taught. He had trained me, however, to keep the cards on my desk from that day forward.

Every dog owner has stories of the cute things their pet did, and we are no different. Our little guy (4.5 pounds fully grown) would intentionally push his toys under the couch so that we would have to retrieve them. This ensured that he then had a playmate holding his toy, which just *had* to be thrown and fetched. He always cooperated when Rosie wanted to dress him up for his birthday, Christmas, Halloween, or for any other occasion. He was a real ham. The thing I remember most was, whenever we announced that it was bedtime, he ran into our bedroom to hide under the bed. He knew he had to sleep in his crate, which was in another room, but - just like any little kid - he figured it was worth a shot to try to stay up.

The joy of this furry blessing lasted for 16 wonderful years.

We made the extremely difficult but medically compassionate decision to put him to sleep two days after his 16th birthday. Kipling's poem filled my head as we took our last ride together to the Mount Laurel Animal Hospital. With all three of us petting him, and with the support of a truly sympathetic staff, he quietly and painlessly left this earth. Kipling questioned why one should "give your heart to a dog to tear," but if you have a dog that you love and enjoy, you already know the answer.

If Heaven is as great as I think it is, God has to have a section for us to throw a ball or two - or He may even have an old account card lying around!

23

Making the Right Choice

The author and his teacher at 97

IT ALL STARTED on March 9, 2017, when I received this Facebook message:

"Are you the Charles Sacchetti who wrote that charming article in the March 6 [issue of *The*] *Philadelphia Inquirer*? If so, my mother was your typing teacher at Bartram High, and [she] sends her regards."

This surprise was from Arlene "Taffy" Rubin, the daughter of my favorite teacher, Gladyce Rubin. Over 50 years had passed since we had seen each other, and her message was a blessing to receive.

Back in 1964, as a senior at Bartram in southwest Philly, my schedule was found to have an open period that I had to fill with an elective course, and I was given a choice of several. When I noticed that one of them was Introduction to Typing, I chose that class for two sound reasons: The first was that although I was enrolled in the college-prep curriculum with the plan to become an accounting major at Temple University, I thought learning to type would be quite helpful moving forward. The second reason - just as important to a red-blooded boy of 17 - was that the class would consist of 35 girls, two of my buddies, and me.

To my surprise, I really enjoyed the course. Mrs. Rubin was an excellent teacher with the demeanor of a loving mother toward all of her kids. She taught us the proper techniques with great patience and expertise. By the time I graduated, I could type about 45 words per minute. I was able to type properly, using all ten digits, unlike my two friends, who developed calluses on their index fingers and stiff necks as they mastered the hunt-and-peck method.

In addition to the obvious benefits of acquiring this skill, an unanticipated perk presented itself to the three of us. Mrs. Rubin was also the dean of admissions, and, as a busy school administrator, she required some volunteer hours from chosen student workers. We three filled that need and, as a result, were able to shuffle our classes so that our work in the office resulted in early dismissal each day.

Taffy's message conjured up many of these wonderful memories, and I just had to see my favorite teacher again, give her a hug, and thank her for teaching me a skill that has proven invaluable throughout both my professional and private life. So, shortly thereafter, the three of us arranged to meet for lunch at Lancers Diner, near Taffy's home. By then, Gladyce was a youthful 96 and, despite some medical issues, still displayed the beautiful nature and charm that had always made spending time with her such a joy.

At lunch, aside from the fun in catching up after all of the years past, a highlight for me was seeing Gladyce so gleefully enjoy her dessert - a strawberry milkshake. But what I remember most about our reunion was the obvious bond of love between mother and daughter. It's clear that Taffy appreciates the treasure with which she has been blessed. Happily, our revived relationship has continued, fed by periodic phone calls and lunch dates which have resulted in the demise of more than a few corned beef sandwiches and other tasty morsels.

On September 16, 2021, I would have loved to see Mrs. Rubin and give her a special hug. However, COVID-19 has caused many altered plans. You see, on that day, Gladyce celebrated her 100th birthday, but the pandemic reduced the major festivities that Taffy had hoped for to a small family gathering. But fear not! For, as soon as can be arranged, I plan to rejoin my favorite teacher for a great lunch - another buffet of laughs, old stories, and a recap of how her big day was spent. And, for dessert, we'll top it all off with a strawberry milkshake!

24

You Can't Take It With You

Let's wrap this up!

ONE THING THAT never ceases to amaze me is how an otherwise good business can have a policy which allows them to treat customers in a way that may jeopardize future patronage. When these practices are easily avoidable but carried out nonetheless, it further boggles my mind. Due to the nature of my work and the fact that we live in an area with a multitude of restaurants, most of these issues have occurred in various eateries. I am not the most patient person on earth by nature, and, although we aren't talking life and death here, I still expect to be treated respectfully when I plunk down my hard-earned money to treat my customer or my family to a meal. However, while a given situation may be aggravating, it can also be humorous.

My wife and I typically go to breakfast after attending Mass on Sundays. We have our favorite spots, but occasionally we'll try someplace new, which was the case on this particular day when we visited a restaurant near our home in New Jersey. Since my wife doesn't drink caffeine, she usually requests hot water with lemon in a coffee cup, and she did so here. The meal was fine, and when we were finished, the waitress handed me the check. I noticed a charge of $1.50 for my wife's cup of hot water. Suspecting a mistake, I questioned the waitress about it, who said the owner required them to charge for hot water because some people bring in their own tea bags. I requested to speak with the boss about it.

When the young manager arrived, he explained that this was the restaurant's policy. I said, "OK, but do you see any used tea bags on the table, and do you realize that your policy isn't appropriate in this case?" He just stood there, silent. I then asked him: If there were cold water in the cup, would there be a charge? He said no. Then, trying to be helpful to this young man, I offered, "Now, if I were to leave after paying for that cup of hot water, I wouldn't be very happy, and I'd probably tell this story to most of my friends, who all live in this area. Plus, I'll never come back here again. Is all of that worth $1.50?" He then relented, no doubt happy to watch us go and wondering why some seemingly normal guy would hassle him about a buck and a half.

I'm sure his confusion would have increased if he learned that we left the waitress a $5 tip for a bill that totaled $9.50! I figured it wasn't her fault, and besides it's a fact of life that service staff usually take the brunt of the anger from the public when situations like this occur, which often means a tiny or nonexistent tip. We did go eat there a few more times, but when we were hit with another $1.50 hot-water fee, I didn't feel like repeating the earlier episode, so I just paid the bill and never returned. By the way, as predicted, all of my friends have heard this story.

While this event was memorable and has gotten its share of laughs over the years, the one I remember most involves the diner on the Pennsylvania side of the bridge. This place had a great salad bar, and the food was always good. It had been recently sold, and I heard that the new owners kept the same chef and menu. However, we soon found out that they obviously made some policy changes - and not for the better. One beautiful summer evening, I decided to take my wife and daughter to this place to enjoy one of their many entrees and delicious desserts. As was the case with the previous owners, the meal included dessert at no additional charge. After dinner, I ordered a slice of carrot cake but decided to take it home for later. The waitress apologetically explained that even though dessert was included in the cost of the meal, the new owners would not allow guests to have it wrapped and take it home.

Here we go again, I thought, *Let me talk to this guy!*

As the new owner approached the table, my wife and daughter braced themselves for what promised to be an interesting discussion. I explained to him that I had visited on many occasions and always enjoyed the meals and salad bar, but I didn't understand why the included dessert couldn't leave the premises unless it was in my stomach. He hemmed and hawed, offering an absurd answer about people wasting food, and this way he could ensure it was eaten. After slapping myself in the head to be sure I heard him right, I asked, "Do you have doggie bags?"

"Sure we do," he replied, "That way the food is not wasted."

I said, "Good. Thank you."

I don't think the owner got my reference when I asked him if we were on *Candid Camera*, although I didn't spot Allen Funt in the restaurant. I thanked him for his time, and he returned to the kitchen. The waitress had been standing nearby the whole time, trying not to laugh out loud. I asked her to bring me the carrot cake and a doggie bag. I took a nibble with my fork while my family and a young couple at the next table enjoyed a hearty laugh, and the rest of my dessert went into the doggie bag, soon to be transported east, as was its destiny!

About a year later, I wasn't surprised to hear that the restaurant was sold again, and I couldn't help but wonder how many other customers, when dessert time came around, were dismayed to find they couldn't take it with them!

25

Earning the Bag

A fitting look

IT SURE SEEMED innocent enough. Recently, I was doing a little YouTube watching and came across an interesting post that immediately got my attention. For some time, I have wondered if it was feasible to make hard-boiled eggs in the microwave. Now, as if by divine providence, I happened upon a video purporting to explain how to do just that, and I only had to invest the five minutes or so to check it out. In the video, an old guy named Harry was standing in his kitchen, telling me how easy it was. He showed me how to put four eggs in a microwave-safe bowl, cover them with water, and add a teaspoon of salt. I wondered why he needed salt, but then Harry explained, very calmly, that the salt would prevent the eggs from going *poof*. He then placed the bowl in the microwave and cooked the eggs on high for eight minutes. After the time passed, he moved them to another bowl of cold water and let them sit for two minutes. Then - presto - he peeled one of those babies, and it looked like a food photo from *Good Housekeeping*.

Heck, I can do that, I thought, *How tough can it be?* What a nice guy he was to show me how to make those tasty, healthy snacks so easily, providing such a positive answer to my long-standing question. *To boot*, I mused, *my wife, LuAnn, will love me for showing her this new cooking technique* - an added bonus, so to speak!

Let me now take the time to explain that I have received very few accolades in the "giving your wife cooking tips" department. Actually, she considers me a menace if I get anywhere near the stove. Her main objection to my culinary attempts is that I am sloppy; I usually spill something, and then I don't clean to her standards, so she has to do it all over again. This is a double-edged sword because she also thinks that I am dish-washing challenged, so she bans me from those too. I must admit, though, that she does have a point, since there is no comparison between my skills around the kitchen and LuAnn's. When she is finished cooking and cleaning, the kitchen looks as pristine as an operating room - hence her desire to keep me away from there except to eat!

But I had a feeling that this morning would be different. Armed with my foolproof technique just learned from old Chef Harry, I wandered into the kitchen to take my first shot at making hard-boiled eggs, microwave style. As I entered, LuAnn asked what I was up to. Noting that she was engrossed with another task in our living room - and not wanting to lie - I simply said, "I'm just going to heat something up, Sweetie." I figured I'd be done in a couple of minutes; then I'd triumphantly show her the finished delicacy, and all would be well.

I retrieved a nice cereal bowl and put only one egg in it, thinking, *Let's not get too crazy on this maiden voyage!* I covered the egg with water as instructed and then added about a quarter teaspoon of sea salt. I placed the bowl into the microwave and covered the top with a paper plate, just in case a little boiling water popped over the edge of the bowl. Since the old guy had cooked four eggs for eight minutes, I reasoned that four minutes ought to be more than enough for one.

I pushed the start button, and the world was peaceful and kind for two minutes and 58 seconds. Then I wondered if I should have used regular salt instead of sea salt when the serenity of the moment was shattered not by the *poof* ol' Harry had described but by the resounding *POP* of my exploding semi-boiled egg. The paper plate blew off, and the inside of the microwave was splattered with shells and equal measures of egg white and yolk.

Startled by the noise, my dear Sicilian wife rushed into the kitchen and assessed the situation, then expressed to me in the loudest and clearest of terms how she regarded my intelligence level and thoughtlessness, despite my sheepish offers to clean up my mess.

After LuAnn ejected me from the kitchen like an umpire throws an unruly manager out of a game, my mind conjured up memories of a football team, the 1980-81 New Orleans Saints. Their record was 1-15 that year, and, during the dismal season, their loyal fans started to call them the New Orleans "'Aints." In fact, they were so embarrassed by the team's performance that they mockingly wore brown paper bags over their heads as they sat in the stands so as not to be recognized while attending the game. Given the trouble, aggravation, and extra work I had caused, I thought my own humorous "bag of shame" might soften my wife's heart the next time our paths crossed.

So I went to my office and fashioned one as best I could. About an hour later, I ventured back upstairs, bag on head, to face the music. LuAnn was silent, but I detected a barely perceptible *smile.*

I'll take it! I thought, and retreated to my office, my bagged head filled with a fresh idea for a story and the self-promise that it'll be "egg beaters" for a while... And that's no yolk!

26

Back on the Road

The author and Mike, the manager

Rosie, Scott Franzke, and John Kruk

IT SURE WAS good, in September of 2019, to continue a tradition that my daughter, Rosanne, and I have been blessed with since 2006. That was the first time we took a father-daughter trip to see the Phillies in spring training at their Clearwater, Florida, complex, and we had a ball. So much so that each year thereafter, we have made plans to see our beloved team play away from home. After six trips to Clearwater, we decided to visit various other cities, among them Chicago and Cleveland. Wherever we go, there are bound to be lots of laughs and lots of food - that's just part of our makeup. My friend, Bill Winarski, has often accompanied us and has been integral to our enjoyment.

I specifically mention Chicago and Cleveland because those sites provided some of our most memorable times. In Chicago in 2012, a few hours before the game with the Cubs at Wrigley Field, we decided to go out for pizza. I really had no idea where to eat, so I paged through the phone book. When I came upon a place called Giordano's and saw that it was in an Italian neighborhood, I surmised that to succeed in such an area, it must serve high-quality pizzas. My hunch paid off. Their Chicago deep dish pizza was so good that I actually inquired about shipping one back to New Jersey, so my wife, LuAnn, could enjoy some. I thought it would be a nice gesture. You see, my wife has no interest in baseball, but she always gives her blessing on our trips so as not to deprive her two baseball nuts of the pleasure. My very sweet idea abruptly soured, however, when the Giordano's manager told me the pizza cost $18 to purchase and another $60 to ship. Sorry, honey!

After the delicious pregame pizza, it was off to Wrigley Field for the night's contest. Rosie is keenly aware that I have a rule that is always in play: If either team is behind by 10 runs, we leave! I can't stand to watch blowouts because the losing team usually gives up anyway. As luck would have it, the Phillies were getting trounced. They were playing sloppily, and the Cubs were hitting the ball all over the place. By the sixth inning, the Phillies were down by nine runs with the Cubs coming to bat. The Cubs scored another run, and, just as I was ready to invoke the 10-run rule, Bill said, "Wait a minute. Chase Utley is leading off in the seventh. If he hits a homer, let's stay." After some prodding by Rosie, and since I sincerely believed that there was no way Chase was going to hit one out that night, I consented. Up to plate stepped Utley and, *bang*, a homer over the right-field fence. Rosie and Bill never let me hear the end of that one while I was forced to endure two more tortuous innings.

Our annual jaunts continued, and, as 2018 rolled around, we decided it was time to go back to spring training after a five-year hiatus. We were all set to leave when, just days before the trip, I took a tumble and badly injured my knee, which required near-immediate surgery and three months of rehab. The much-anticipated trip was off. We agreed that in 2019, we would return to Cleveland to watch the Phillies play the Indians. The plan also included another visit to the Rock and Roll Hall of Fame, and, since the story of our renowned Chicago pregame pizza had resurfaced over the years, I asked Rosie to find out if there were any Giordano's restaurants in the vicinity.

By that time, Giordano's had greatly expanded their market and were located in multiple cities. Sure enough, we found one in Canton, Ohio, about 60 miles from our hotel. You may think you'd have to be a little nuts to drive so far just for a pizza. Well, I wouldn't pay the 60 bucks to ship one home, but taking a 60-mile ride on a beautiful fall day with my equally pizza-loving daughter was an easy decision. In fact, we had the timing planned perfectly - one hour to get there, an hour and a half at the restaurant, one hour to return to the hotel, and arrive at the stadium in plenty of time for the game.

Upon arrival at the pizzeria, we recognized the welcome

Giordano's sign, entered, sat down, and placed our order with Krissy, our server: a medium create-your-own deep dish - half plain for Rosie and half pepperoni for me. After waiting 30 minutes, my highly developed pizza instincts told me that something was amiss. However, since the place was crowded, and the pies were cooked with TLC, I thought there was no reason to panic. Twenty minutes later, everybody who came in after us was eating. I called our waitress over and said hopefully, "Krissy, God has only given me so many heartbeats, and I'm afraid I may run out of them before this pizza gets here." She smiled and went to check on our pie. When Krissy returned with an apologetic look on her face, she explained that the baker had mistakenly topped the whole pie with pepperoni. Rosie was out of luck.

Just then, as if on cue, along came the general manager, Mike Tepe, a very nice guy who looked more like a linebacker for the Browns than the head honcho. Mike apologized profusely for the mishap and offered to cover our bill and even make Rosie a whole new plain pie, just the way she likes it. Knowing we were pressed for time, he brought out my pizza, so I could dig in, and made a nice salad for Rosie while she waited for her pie, which arrived 10 minutes later. Both Krissy and Mike checked on us several times, and Mike assured me that the meal was on Giordano's. He just asked that I take care of Krissy, which I was more than happy to do. Mike, an excellent manager, did everything he could to successfully turn a bad situation into an enjoyable visit.

Now, that's what I call customer service!

Naturally, we had more than half of both pizzas left, so I asked

Krissy to wrap them in foil for us. Back to the hotel we went and promptly placed our pies into the refrigerator. The following day, we headed home after lovingly packing the leftovers in our cooler with plenty of ice. When we arrived, LuAnn finally got to taste and enjoy that great pizza, albeit seven years later than I had hoped.

As for the games at Cleveland, the Phillies dropped two out of three. It wasn't so bad, though - Rosie got on TV Friday night, in the eighth inning, as the camera panned for people wearing Phillies "regalia." On Sunday, just before the game, while walking in the corridor, she spotted Phillies announcers John Kruk and Scott Franzke, rushed over to them, and "suggested" they pose for a photo with her. I quickly said, "Smile," as she nudged her 5'4" self between those two big guys. The camera *clicked* and - bingo! - another perfect memory.

27

A Command Performance

Sam (right), age 93, at buddy Fred's 101st birthday party, 2016

I CLEARLY REMEMBER the first time I met Sam Nasuti at his "big brother's" birthday party in January of 2014. The festivities took place at the Masonic Village in Burlington, New Jersey. Sam was one of the honored guests, there to celebrate his pal Fred Frett's 99th birthday. "Uncle Fred" was the uncle of my dear friend and former Temple University baseball teammate, Ted Frett. As a beloved second father to Ted, my friend's devotion to his uncle was a natural outgrowth of their relationship.

Sam was a spry 91 when we met, and his initial reticence

toward me melted quickly as we began chatting. Our conversation flowed easily from his south Philadelphia roots to the Phillies and finally moved on to the topic that really made his motor run: his career in music. Sam was a professional singer and musician from the age of 17, and he had actually started performing at the age of six, singing at family functions to the loving applause of his relatives. Sam's work had taken him all over the country, enabling him to rub elbows with the biggest stars of the music world. A self-taught pianist, he didn't bother reading music; he was able to play beautifully by ear. In other words, he had the innate ability, without the benefit of sheet music, to reproduce a piece after hearing it - a rare skill indeed. Even at his advanced age, it wasn't uncommon to find Sam playing a few tunes on one of the pianos located in a lounge area of the Masonic Home.

Sam was not a reluctant name-dropper. He was very proud of his career and had an abundance of stories about meeting and working with the likes of Nat King Cole, Tony Bennett, and Dean Martin - whom he described as being a "really nice guy." Sam was, however, very quick to give his opinion of another icon which surprised me. A colleague once offered to introduce him to Frank Sinatra, but previously Sam had seen Ol' Blue Eyes in a heated discussion with a band member, and he considered Frank's unwarranted behavior to be bullyish, so he politely refused the introduction. I suppose that would put Sam in a very small club indeed, but he wore that refusal as a badge of honor. One story that I found particularly poignant was when he shared that a young Billie Holiday literally "cried on [his] shoulder on the front steps" of a hotel to which she was refused admission in the segregated South.

I regarded my visits with Ted to see his uncle as a real privilege. I had even taken the opportunity to visit both Fred and Sam solo, sometimes crashing their "lunch gang," which consisted of the same four cronies for years. I especially appreciated the honor of being invited to each of Uncle Fred's subsequent birthday parties following the one in 2014. In fact, on Saturday, January 18th, 2020, Ted and the family honored Uncle Fred on birthday number 105. Of course, Sam - then age 97 - was in attendance, and we had the opportunity to sit and talk a little baseball, music, and tell the kinds of stories that usually creep into the conversation when two Italian buddies get together. Although confined to a wheelchair, Sam was still dapper, wearing his signature baseball cap and windbreaker.

As the party progressed, the time came for Ted's 11 grandkids to put on their yearly "talent show" under the watchful eyes of Grandmom - Ted's wife, Judy - and the mothers, Jenny Butler and Christie Frett. Uncle Fred, Sam, and the others happily looked on as they were serenaded by all of the little ones, who opened with the national anthem and continued to some more recent songs. When their performance wound to a close, the show-biz bug bit Sam big time. He belted out an old standard, "It's a Sin to Tell a Lie," and was quickly joined by Judy and Christie. Their impromptu harmonizing was a sight (and sound) to behold. We were all amazed at 97-year-old Sam's vocal strength and flawless delivery. When he broke into his second song, "This Can't Be Love," Sam was in a world of his own. Now the only singer, the lyrics and melody flowed effortlessly from him, and the audience was spellbound. I was still marveling at the strength and power of his delivery when he finished, and applause filled the room.

With the show over, it was time for the coffee and cake. Few people noticed, but, about 15 minutes after his performance, Sam slowly slumped in his chair. With the thoughtfulness of a true family protector, Ted calmly wheeled Sam out of the room and toward the nurses' station. When they arrived, it was apparent that Sam had stopped breathing. He was taken to the hospital, where he peacefully died in the wee hours of Sunday morning. When Ted informed Uncle Fred that his buddy had passed away, Fred said without hesitation, "That's just the way he would want to go."

The definition of a "command performance" is a "presentation of a play, concert, opera, or other show at the request of royalty." There certainly were no typical kings or queens present at that birthday party, but the King of Kings surely was. Sam's God-given gift was shared once more with a loving audience. And Sam's other great gift, that of true friendship, was again shared after a brief hiatus when Fred joined him in Paradise just five months later, on June 11th.

May they both rest in peace.

28

Words Undying

The author with his dad

IT NEVER CEASES to amaze me how I can remember certain words, said to me long ago, by friends and relatives. Whether uttered during times of stress, joy, or just plain old conversation, for some reason, they continue to live in my memory. And these sage-like phrases pop up involuntarily, every once in a while, when they are apropos to the situation.

For instance, my mother would frequently say, "You get what you pay for," when she bought something for the house. Back then, Wanamaker's was her store of choice. Although they were a bit more pricey than other sources when it came to furniture or other big-ticket items, Mom always believed that she got the best bang for her buck there. The service and guarantees Wanamaker's offered proved to be good investments and, to her, money well spent. Her pet phrase came to my mind again 46 years ago, when it was time for my new bride and me to buy bedroom and dining room furniture. We spent a little more than we wanted to, but we still have that furniture today, and it looks great. Thanks, Mom.

In the early '70s, my boss at Temple University's athletic department was Ernie Casale, the best and most heralded athletic director the school has ever known. He would say to me, his youngest staff member at the time, "When you do something, do it first class." That summarized how he conducted himself and ran his department. I've remembered those words over the years and have come to understand what Ernie meant: What we do professionally directly affects how we are perceived. If we do things in a slipshod manner, we cannot command the respect of others. Those words helped me to be more thorough in my professional life and especially in my subsequent sales career.

A few years later, another Temple boss, Lloyd Eslinger, the director of facilities, gave me what may be the most important advice in very few words. As I was struggling with a personnel problem involving one of my assistants, Lloyd said, "When you're faced with two possible decisions, usually the one that is the toughest to make is the right one." Over the years, this has proven to be true, and I have shared this guidance with my friends and family.

In the early '80s, it was my privilege to be mentored by a wonderful man, Lamarr Dobbs. He was the corporate sales manager of our small company, which manufactured specialty and industrial chemicals. Lamarr had a unique management style, and his keen perception in all situations led me to suspect that he could actually read my mind! He was always there if I needed help and pushed me to my limits to enable me to succeed. He had a great, dry sense of humor, and he would tell all of the guys that if we could give him an excuse that he hadn't heard before, he'd give us a dollar!

One day, when I first started working in the field with him, Lamarr gave me a line that I have never forgotten. I had made the common mistake of talking to the customer when I should have been listening, and I blew the sale. As I walked with him back to my car, I tried to justify what happened with a plausible answer. But he just looked at me, smiled, and said, "That's not worth a dollar." I learned, from that moment on, to talk less and listen more.

As I recall all of this wisdom, handed down to me from many different sources, I especially remember some words told to me by my dear father, Henry. Dad was at once sensitive and tough, strong and self-educated. His words of "enlightenment" were always greatly considered by my sister, Kathy, and me, as you might expect in a typical Italian-American home. When I was 17, I had just received my learner's permit and was only allowed to drive if accompanied by a licensed driver in the front seat. So, on this particular Saturday morning, I asked Dad if we could go for a spin, which would mark our maiden voyage. I was happy to hear his response in the affirmative.

I backed our Ford Fairlane out of our southwest Philly row-home's garage. Upon entering Buist Avenue, I made a right turn. With my light green, as I attempted to make a right turn at the corner of 65th Street, a red Mustang bolted from my left and ran the red light, forcing me to jam on the brakes. In my father's inimitable style, he delivered the words that live in me today and that have served me well, especially during my out-side-sales days when I regularly drove over 35,000 miles per year. Not sounding at all like Ward Cleaver or Cliff Huxtable, but instead clearly demonstrating his south Philly upbringing, Dad turned to me and uttered these profound words:

"Kid, when you drive, you gotta have eyes in your ass."

Despite the anatomical impossibility, his advice has proven to be true many times in the 50-plus years that have passed.

Thanks, Dad.

CPSIA information can be obtained
at www.ICGtesting.com
Printed in the USA
BVHW052030170122
626439BV00019B/641